BIBLICAL MEDITATIONS
FOR THE
EASTER SEASON

Biblical Meditations
for the
Easter Season

by
Carroll Stuhlmueller, C.P.

Introduction by
Most Rev. Charles A. Buswell
Bishop of Pueblo, Colorado

PAULIST PRESS
New York/Ramsey

Library of Congress
Catalog Card Number: 80-81030

ISBN: 0-8091-2283-9

Published by Paulist Press
545 Island Road, Ramsey, N.J. 07446

Printed and bound in the
United States of America

Contents

To
Lisa and John Lacci
Mike, Bill and Kevin McCune
a small remembrance
for many joys and hopes

Foreword

The Bible was lived long before it was written. This book of *Biblical Meditations* endeavors to put the words of the Scriptures back into our life *for the Easter Season.*

Even after the Bible was inscribed on stone tablets or on parchment and papyrus scrolls, people normally did not read the Bible. They listened to its proclamation. This announcement during liturgical assemblies always included explanation, application and decision making. We are told, for instance:

> Ezra read plainly from the book of the law of God, *interpreting it so that all could understand* what was read (Neh 10:8).

Understanding did not consist simply in reconstructing the historical setting nor in proving that it once really happened. Rather the people were drawn to confirm, validate and live anew what once happened among their ancestors. Understanding, therefore, meant reexperiencing biblical inspiration and living by the Holy Spirit. The Bible was to happen *now,* as a well-known passage of Deuteronomy insists upon. Several centuries after Moses' death, he summons his followers and speaks again, this time by the Levites:

> Hear, O Israel, the statutes and decrees which I proclaim in your hearing *this day,* that you may learn them and take care to observe them. The Lord, our God, made a covenant *with us* at Ho-

reb [= Sinai], not with our ancestors ... but
with us, all of us who are alive here this day
(Deut 5:1–3).

Listening in this way relived the experience of Sinai.
It also demanded the same response of love and loyalty.
When the people assembled at the sanctuary of Shechem
for renewing the covenant, life-decisions were at stake.
All their nerves were tense with the excitement and ex-
pectation as the preacher called out at Shechem:

Now, therefore, fear the Lord and serve him
completely and sincerely.... Decide today
whom you will serve.... As for me and my
household, we will serve the Lord (Josh 24:14–
15).

The entire liturgical setting of this twenty-fourth
chapter of *Joshua* provides the steps for our own *Biblical
Meditations.* First, we are conscious of our church at
prayer; we are not loners (Josh 24:1). Second, we hear the
wonderful deeds which the Lord accomplished for our
ancestors (Josh 24:2–13). Third, we appropriate and endorse the faith of our mothers and fathers (Josh 24:14–
15). Fourth, it is necessary that we realize the implications and seriously accept all the consequences in our daily life (Josh 24:16–24). Fifth, we celebrate the decision
solemnly within the community of the Church, intensely
conscious of God's presence with us (Josh 24:25–27).
Last of all, we return to our daily life, interiorly transformed so that our smallest actions reflect our vigorous
faith.

Like a previous *Biblical Meditations for Lent,* this
book for the Easter season follows many of the stages of

prayer and decision just outlined from Joshua Chapter 24. The biblical selections are provided by the Church's cycle of readings for the seven weeks of the Easter season. These ought to be read in their entirety from the Bible or from a missal. In case that is not possible, a summary is provided which highlights one or two key phrases or ideas. The reader may want to add or substitute other points which the Holy Spirit inspires from the biblical passages for the day.

The meditation is born from that fertile moment of combining the inspiration of the first Bible passage with the second Bible passage (and on Sundays with the third). Each reenforces and enriches the other in such a way that a new insight is conceived. This perception grows within a contemporary setting, absorbs influences from modern life and in turn directs that life as God desires. Decisions are reached or confirmed. The final prayer with each meditation is usually drawn from the antiphonal psalm after the first reading in the missal or lectionary. What we seek most of all, however, is not decisions nor even a better life, but the appreciation of God's holy and wonderful presence with us. We wait upon the Lord and renew our strength (Is 40:31).

These reflections hopefully will have enough life to spring the reader loose to adapt and relive each passage of the Bible, each person in his/her own way but always in loving communion with all their brothers and sisters in the Church and in the entire world.

Because the meditations in this book flow from life, they were influenced consciously and subconsciously by people important in my own life. I single out at this time the family of my sister Vera and her husband, Joseph M. McCune. To their children I dedicate with love this small sign of appreciation and hope.

I am grateful as well to Bishop Charles A. Buswell of Pueblo, Colorado, for his Introduction. His leadership, vision and courage have reached across our country and embody the kind of Church where the strength and graciousness of the Bible live in a most challenging way. He enables great ideas to be at home in the traditions of the Church.

The manuscript was completed while lecturing at St. Charles Archdiocesan Seminary, Philadelphia, and at Holy Cross Benedictine Abbey, Cañon City, Colorado. The kindness experienced in each place blessed me and my work. Another word of gratitude is owed to Sister Margaret Brosile, C.S.J., of the Mary Louis Academy, Jamaica, N.Y. The joy of her heart and of her apostolate in teaching music, as well as her friendship through the years, turned the chore of her typing a difficult manuscript into an ever-grateful memory for me. I am indebted to Fr. Kenneth O'Malley, C.P., Director of Library at the Catholic Theological Union, for proofreading the manuscript and for preparing the indices. In this instance, as in many others, he expended his energy and talents with abundant good humor. This meditation book, as well as the preceding one for Lent, traces its origin to the request and encouragement of Mr. Robert Heyer of Paulist Press.

Most of all, may our common meditation upon God's word seal our hearts with the pledge of the Holy Spirit who reinspires the Bible in us and within our Church today.

> The Spirit makes intercession for us with groanings that cannot be expressed in speech. The one who searches hearts knows what the Spirit

means, for the Spirit intercedes for the saints as
God wills (Rom 8:26–27).

Carroll Stuhlmueller, C.P.
The Catholic Theological Union at Chicago

Introduction

In his opening address at the Second Vatican Council, Pope John XXIII spoke about the "prophets of gloom". They seem always to be with us, Pope John said; and they are always forecasting disaster. Pope John disagreed. He had a firm trust in Divine Providence. He had great confidence in the Holy Spirit. God would guide things well according to His own wonderful designs.

I subscribe to Pope John's sentiments. Prophets of gloom are still with us. But hopeful signs abound. One of the most hopeful of these is the loving and generous response people everywhere are giving to the Word of God. It is no longer unusual for Roman Catholic Christians to read faithfully, even daily, the Bible. Nearly every parish in the United States has one or more Bible study groups. Prayer groups are common, all centering their prayer on Holy Scripture, the Living Word.

I had a 'scriptural conversion' during the Second Vatican Council. As preparations were being made to debate the schema which was then known as the "Sources of Revelation", I joined the bishops of the United States in a study group. Cardinal Albert Meyer of Chicago was the motivating force. Father Barnabas Ahern, C.P., was our teacher. I came to an understanding of the beauty and of the power of God's Word that I had never had before. I began to see in Holy Scripture the actual presence of the Lord. I began to realize that while pondering this Word, the power of God and of His love would sink deep into my mind and heart to transform me into the kind of person my Christian vocation called me to be.

It was Cardinal Bea who was a special source of inspiration to me as we discussed Divine Revelation during the Vatican Council sessions. Eighty-two years of age, he had just been named the head of the Secretariat for Promoting Christian Unity. He had been the Rector of the Pontifical Biblical Institute in Rome. He lived out in his own life the full power of the Gospel which he knew so well. Cardinal Bea brought to the discussions an open spirit and a desire that the Bible become a rich source of spiritual nourishment for all. That spirit prevailed as the Dogmatic Constitution on Divine Revelation was approved. That same spirit now permeates the entire Church.

At the time the discussions mentioned above were carried out, there were large posters around the city of Rome advertising the British European Airways, BEA. It is said that someone took one of these posters and hung it over the door of the Pontifical Biblical Institute. It read: "Travel with BEA". I am pleased that the post-Vatican II Church has heeded this advice!

I am delighted that Father Carroll Stuhlmueller, C.P., has invited me to write a brief introduction to his timely book, *Biblical Meditations for the Easter Season.* This book follows his *Biblical Meditations for Lent* which has been a source of spiritual nourishment for many. It, like its predecessor, will give generous encouragement to Bible reading as the Dogmatic Constitution on Divine Revelation asks. It will also aid those who read the Bible to come to it, in the words of R.A.F. MacKenzie, S.J., "with faith in Christ, who is the last and definitive utterance of God's word; with faith in the Church, which is the depository and custodian of that word; and with faith in the Scripture itself, which is the expression in human language of the message delivered by God".

The present volume follows the cycle of liturgical

readings for Sundays and weekdays from Easter to Pentecost. This provides the reader with a practical format for daily prayer, reflecting on the Word of God in keeping with the spirit of the Church during the Easter season. The selection of readings touches all the bases of the spiritual life. Since the readers do not pick and choose these readings, they are called on to ponder those that are probably more necessary for their growth and development. Moreover, these readings are the ones used by the entire Church. The individual reader will be in touch with the Church throughout the world and will feel a bond of solidarity with the entire Body of Christ.

Someone has said that a good homilist should preach with the Bible in one hand and with the daily newspaper in the other. Father Stuhlmueller's *Biblical Meditations* has something like this in mind: the focus is on the Word of God and on praying this Word; yet always in the context of contemporary real-life situations.

Every Christian is called to grow personally into Christ's likeness; and the entire Christian family is challenged to grow into the fulness of the stature of Christ. Father Carroll is a part of that growth process. I am glad that he has shared with us a sure way of making that growth happen. I trust that many will be helped greatly to come to, or to advance in, Christian maturity as they make use of *Biblical Meditations for the Easter Season*.

† Charles A. Buswell
Bishop of Pueblo

PART ONE

Weekdays of the
Easter Season

Easter Monday

Acts 2:14, 22–32. Peter declares that Jesus suffered "by
the set purpose . . . of God" and at the hands of pagans
ignorant of God's plans. Through his sufferings and
resurrection the prophecies are fulfilled.

Matt 28:8–15. Women-witnesses carry Jesus' instructions
to the disciples that they "are to go to Galilee, where
they will see him."

According to Peter's discourse on Pentecost, spoken
under the impact of the Holy Spirit, all the prophecies,
plans and "set purpose" of God converged upon the sufferings, death and resurrection of Jesus. The master-plan
of world salvation moved forward with inexorable determination and "when the designated time had come, God
sent forth his Son born of a woman" (Gal 4:4). This magnificent, focal point of God's wisdom involved the "pagans [who were] to crucify and kill him." Everyone, then
believers and unbelievers, people who acted ignorantly or
cunningly, impulsively or deliberately, with good or bad
intentions, were caught up in this supreme purpose of
God for the universe.

> God has given us the wisdom to understand
> fully the mystery, the plan he was pleased to de-
> cree in Christ, to be carried out in the fullness
> of time: namely, to bring all things in the heav-
> ens and on earth into one under Christ's head-
> ship (Eph 1:9–10).

Yet, the overpowering wonder of this mystery was
not intended to stop the clock and paralyze us to the
point of immobility, nor to stun us beyond words. The

disciples were not told by the women to build a shrine around the Holy Sepulchre and make it an object of world pilgrimage. They were summoned away from Jerusalem, and were told "to go [up north] to Galilee, where they will see him" and receive further instruction about preaching this message to the whole world.

The disciples were to plunge into this world plan of God. By their teaching, men and women will be absorbed within a rhythm that leads to suffering and death, giving up everything for the kingdom (Luke 9:23–27) and living totally by faith. That same rhythm also included a movement toward resurrection and eternal life (Luke 18:22). The years after the death and resurrection of Jesus were to stretch over a longer period of time than that from Abraham (who lived around 1850 B.C.) to the fullness of time when Jesus appeared, born of a woman.

As disciples, we are to dedicate and use all of our human resources for the kingdom of God. We must firmly believe that we are part of a plan beyond human comprehension. We are to display exceptional ingenuity but most of all we are to manifest *faith*, that firm confidence that our human life will be transformed according to the likeness of Jesus' resurrection (Rom 6:5). We must never allow any momentary triumph or defeat, even the empty tomb of Jesus, to distract us from keeping our eyes on Jesus, our ears attuned to faith, our heart compassionate toward the world, our hope beyond the reach of frustration and anger. No rumors, lies and scandals will detour us, no human attempts at explanation, no payoffs, no bribery will compromise us. All this falls within God's world plan.

"Do not be afraid! Go and carry the news to my brothers and sisters" across the world!

Prayer:

> I set the Lord ever before me;
>> with him at my right hand I shall not be
>> disturbed.
> Keep me safe, O God;
>> you are my hope.

Easter Tuesday

Acts 2:36–41. Repent and be baptized. It was to you and your children that the promise was made, and to all those still far off whom the Lord our God calls.

John 20:11–18. In appearing to Mary Magdalene Jesus instructs her to "go to my brothers and sisters and tell them, 'I am ascending to my Father and your Father.' "

We must seek for Jesus and long for his presence. Yet we cannot find him unless he first finds us. Only when Jesus appeared to Mary Magdalene and spoke her name, "Mary!" a word that reached into the heart and mind and illumined her whole self, only then did Mary discover Jesus with love and veneration.

To be found by Jesus, we must accept Jesus on *his* terms. Mary would never have found Jesus unless he first spoke her name. Yet, even at such an ecstatic moment, Jesus did not permit Mary to cling to him. "Rather," he said, "go to my brothers and sisters and tell them, 'I am ascending to my Father and your Father.' " To be found by Jesus demands a continuing attitude of obedient faith. Jesus finds us not that we may selfishly possess him but that we may share this joy with many others. We must, in a sense, lose it, in order to be found again by Jesus in the community of faith. Mary was first ridiculed by the disciples when she reported the marvelous event of Jesus' resurrection.

To be found by Jesus we must accept God on *his* terms. Obedient faith not only means unselfish sharing of God's gift with others, but like Peter we must also turn to the Scriptures. During his address to the people on Pentecost, Peter stated that "it was to you and your children that the promise was made." This promise motivated Moses, David and all the prophets. Yet, the Scriptures, which the people knew all along, did not of themselves provide the clue and the meaning of Jesus in their lives. The Bible had to be read in the light of Jesus' resurrection. The same is true of Jesus' earthly life. No matter how marvelous it was, "with signs and wonders," it still remained insufficient of itself. Therefore, Jesus tells Mary Magdalene not to cling to him, for I have not yet ascended to the Father. She is given the special commission to tell the disciples that Jesus must ascend to his Father and their Father, to his God and their God. Earthly existence needs to be seen as a way reaching beyond human vision.

To be found by Jesus, then, we must allow our hearts and minds to be flooded with a light beyond our control and comprehension. Hours of prayer and contemplation are necessary. The obedience with which we follow God's will in our daily life must become the law of our prayer. After reading the Bible, we need to pause, remain silent, and wait upon God's revelation. Within this silence, everything merges into a single response, whether it be our study of the Bible, our daily life with its problems and hopes, or our conversation with others and the personal presence of Jesus. We live in the light of Christ

(John 8:12). We read the Bible with new wisdom, we address our hopes and problems with new vitality, and we are more faithful disciples of the Lord.

Like Mary Magdalene we return to our family and exclaim: I have seen the Lord! He has found me and spoken my name.

Prayer:

> See, the eyes of the Lord are upon those who
>   fear him,
>   upon those who hope for his kindness.
> Our soul waits for the Lord,
>   who is our help and our shield.
> The earth is full of the goodness of the Lord.

Easter Wednesday

Acts 3:1–10. Peter cures the crippled man who then jumped about, praising God within the temple.

Luke 24:13–35. Jesus catches up with two disciples on their way to Emmaus; and at the breaking of the bread he disappears.

Jesus enables us, his people, to make our way through life more confidently and more joyfully, with clearer purpose and meaning. He cured the impaired limbs of the temple beggar, whose crippled feet and ankles prevented him from walking. Jesus healed the darkened, discouraged minds of the two disciples who had felt betrayed by Jesus' death, had given up and were now returning to their former way of life. As a result of Jesus' presence and powerful word, they were able to face life with renewed vigor and enthusiasm.

The presence of Jesus along the way of life shows up in still other ways. Jesus draws upon the Scriptures of his ancestors, their Torah, prophets and other writings, in order to explain how it was necessary for the Messiah "to undergo all this [suffering and death] so as to enter into his glory." All through the history of the chosen people, God was not only carefully guiding the people in their everyday life but he was also providing a deeper purpose. He was continually giving signals of how the Messiah was to live, preach, suffer, die and rise again from the dead. Every event of human history, then, had a meaning in itself but it also contained a mystical, deeper significance that would be appreciated only through Jesus. In order for us to read the Scriptures with this fuller wisdom, we need to recognize the presence of Jesus with us. Then we too will exclaim as did the disciples: "Were not our hearts burning inside us as he talked to us on the road and explained the Scriptures to us?"

The great moments of sacred history, reaching back to Moses and Abraham, as well as the striking ways in which Jesus responded to people's needs and hopes with words and actions, comforting, instructing and healing, all this material has provided the basic material for church worship and liturgical ceremonies. By processions we relive the times when Jesus walked along, for instance to Emmaus, or when the Israelites made forced marches through the desert; by sacred meals we commemorate the manna with which God fed the Israelites in the desert (Ex 16:14–36) and made a sacred covenant with them (Ex 24:1–11). At the Eucharist we also recall how Jesus fed the multitudes in the desert (John 6) and sealed a new covenant with his disciples (Luke 22:20). Today's gospel recalls the full setting of the Eucharist: first the reading of Scripture and its explanation in terms of the contemporary moment, then the ritual of the sacred meal, finally at the time of consecration and communion, Jesus physically disappeared because he was there symbolically under the form of bread.

All of life's journeys are reactivated in the moment of liturgy and prayer. The Eucharist on its part prepares us to return to daily life with a more sensitive awareness of Jesus' presence. By profound experience of God at prayer and the reading of Scripture, we become all the more conscious of Jesus' otherwise hidden presence in all the other moments of life. With renewed faith, we ought to be able to look *hopefully* and *enthusiastically* at life all about us.

Some important questions come to mind. Do we believe that Jesus can take our most crippled moments and transform them into great possibilities? Do we believe that Jesus can work miracles today? Are we able to slough off discouragement and frustration and vigorously turn ourselves around and return to the holy city of divine accomplishments?

Prayer:

God, you remember forever your covenant, made with our ancestors on Mount Sinai, renewed with us in the Eucharist. You remember us, each moment, wherever we are. Therefore, the earth is full of your goodness. We look to you, O Lord, in your strength; we seek to serve you constantly. We sing to you and proclaim all your wondrous deeds.

Easter Thursday

Acts 3:11–26. A crowd gathered in the temple at the miraculous cure of the lame man. Peter addressed them, admitting that they handed Jesus over "out of ignorance." Yet all of Scripture pointed to Jesus' death and resurrection.

Luke 24:35–48. Jesus appeared, showed his hands and feet and stressed that "the Messiah must suffer and rise from the dead." "Thus it is written."

Two, almost contradictory ideas join together: on the one hand, the ignorant, impulsive and angry reaction of the crowds in demanding Jesus' death, and on the other hand the long, careful and determined planning on God's part.

Speaking to the people, Peter declared: "All the prophets who have spoken from Samuel onward have announced the events of these days." Jesus said to the disciples as he appeared to them on the first Easter evening: "Recall those words I spoke to you when I was still with you: everything written about me in the law of Moses and the prophets and psalms had to be fulfilled." These passages are not to be interpreted to mean that specific details had been predicted ahead of time, like the place of his birth or the nailing to a cross. Texts in the Bible like Micah 5:1–3 or Psalm 22:17–19 would have been fulfilled, if Jesus had been poor and lowly of the family of David (which came true because Joseph was his foster-father) or if Jesus had been identified with suffering and oppressed people, longing for God to send relief and peace. Understood in this larger sense, the Scriptures kept alive a conviction and a faith, not only that God lovingly saves us in our destitution and desperation, but also that God uses these means to exercise extraordinary power and transform our existence.

Fulfillment of Scripture then does not normally consist in verbal prediction and specific implementation at a later date. Rather, fulfillment is to be applied to a long, continuous attitude of faith, whereby generations of people find their hopes sustained, their trials overcome, their worship directed, their laws and customs purified, their lives ever more dedicated to God. We too must identify ourselves with all "this cloud of witnesses" (Heb 12:1). We in turn, as Jesus said to the disciples, must become "witnesses to all this" to our generation.

If God's plans and predictions are so thoroughly enmeshed in human existence, if they are fulfilled in the long sweep and continuous rhythm of faith, then we should not be surprised if they include such ungodly elements as human ignorance, even sinfulness and ruthlessness. Peter admitted this fact very openly: the people acted "out of ignorance." It is far easier for us to admit that our lives are swept along by divine providence, than to agree that divine providence includes such unlikely features as ignorance and malice.

In fact, ignorance is probably the most difficult aspect of all. God, we feel, can summon his might and strike down evil people and overcome their evident wickedness, but what can God do about ignorance! He can hardly punish a person for doing something unknowingly! And often it is more difficult to reason with an ignorant person than with someone deliberately doing what is wrong. Yet, to redeem us in a human way, God had to accept this most human situation, ignorance!

Ignorance has to be dealt with, not ignored! First of all, we ought not to feel helpless at our naive, unenlightened and impulsive actions. God will not allow us to be condemned for what we never intended to do, yet actually did impulsively and thoughtlessly. God asks us to be peaceful in the face of many events outside of our control. We live in a world where many people of good will act in ways that are harmful to us or at least that make our own existence difficult to manage. The Scriptures remind us that the redemption of the world by Jesus Christ was achieved within the ignorant and impulsive actions of many people. God will accomplish the same wonder for us. In our bewilderment we need to turn ever more often to the Scriptures, to see a divine direction within such human situations.

Prayer:

Lord, who are we that you should be mindful of us and care for us? We feel humiliated by the greatness of the stars and the roar of the wind. We are discouraged by world forces beyond our control. We are humiliated at the ignorant things we do. Yet, Jesus, you surround us with glory and honor, give us rule over the works of your hands, over sheep and oxen and the beasts of the field. O Lord, our God, how wonderful is your name in all the earth!

Easter Friday

Acts 4:1–12. Peter and John were arrested for causing a
   commotion through the miracle of curing a lame man
   and for preaching the resurrection. Peter replied that
   in no other name but that of Jesus are people saved.

John 21:1–14. In this appendix to John's gospel, the
   disciples are again in Galilee, at their trade of fishing.
   Jesus appeared and called them to a miraculous haul of
   fishes.

The disciples are back again where they started: in
Galilee at their trade of fishing. Yet, a tremendous difference is also to be noticed. They recognized Jesus at once,
obediently followed his advice, hauled in one hundred
and fifty-three fish, and ate with Jesus.

Many important or at times incidental traits of earlier life contribute now to the apostolate. Jesus' disciples
realize better their place in the church, and the meaning
of the Eucharist. They are called to fish for men and
women, and through Jesus there will be an abundant
number of converts. Even Peter's trait of a natural, impulsive leader—in earlier days a source of annoyance and
also of joy as well as a way of settling arguments and
questions with dispatch—now confirms Jesus' plan for
Peter to be the rock and principal leader of the Church.

Other details of life, which people are tempted to
cast aside as useless or meaningless, are turned by God
into important aspects of their future existence. "The
stone which the builders rejected has become the cornerstone."

The cure of a lame man at the temple gate catches
the melody and dance of prophetic announcements (Is
35:5–6). The new Jerusalem appears, with people wor-

shiping God joyfully and enthusiastically. Fish becomes a symbol of eucharistic devotion within the new holy city.

This pattern by which God picks up incidental details of human existence and transforms them into key aspects of the future or into a cornerstone upon which to rest an entire edifice provides us with much encouragement and a stern warning. There are casual, random, and seemingly irrelevant events. Small opportunities come and go. Small people, again with little significance for ourselves, pass us by each day. Lame people are carried along, unable to catch up with us, liable to be overlooked by ourselves in our hurry about "important" matters! Routine actions, like our normal employment with its day by day sameness, become so monotonous that we perform the actions like a machine, and treat others just as impersonally in our employment.

Yet, God can take advantage of such details to drastically change our existence. Something, at the distant outer circle of our needs and interests, can move to the center and support everything else.

First of all, these Scripture passages based on the example of Jesus and on God's ways through the ages advise us to respect *all* life, even the tiniest piece of it. We can never brush off people because they are poor, of no clout, boring and troublesome. They may be the lame person at the gate of the temple, looking to us for alms. Yet, if we strike up a friendship and act not only humanly but with the charity of Jesus and his compassion, this person may be the cause of an entirely new outlook on life. At times, a child who is crippled in mind or in body becomes the rallying point of the entire family, the catalyst of extraordinary goodness in them, the reason for their strong family bond.

Then too just as the disciples returned to their native country of Galilee and to their old trade of fishing, so too we must never deny our ancestry or heritage. We are never to be ashamed of our past nor feel crippled because of it. Again here is where we gain the assurance, so important for our own strong peace of mind and for our encouraging attitude toward others, that God does work miracles. We can impart that reassuring advice: "God makes all things work together for the good of those who have been called according to his decree" (Rom 8:28).

Finally, it is faith in Jesus which turns the most inconsequential aspects of our life into cornerstones for our future, the source of our greatest joy, the roots of our eternal happiness.

Prayer:

Each day let me say: "This is the day the Lord has made; let us be glad and rejoice in it." Let me look upon each person, even the one who might rush past me, as your favorite one, sent to me for a special purpose. Give me the peaceful assurance that really and truly *everything* works together for my good. The stone which is liable to be rejected you make into a cornerstone of my everlasting joy.

Easter Saturday

Acts 4:13–21. When Peter and John were prohibited from speaking in the name of Jesus, they replied that God must be obeyed, not human beings. The priests and elders could not explain how a miracle took place, nor would they accept its consequences that Jesus was the Messiah.

Mark 16:9–15. Jesus appeared to the Eleven and reprimanded them for refusing to accept the witness of Mary Magdalene and the two others on their way to the country.

Both the Jewish Sanhedrin, the supreme ruling body of Judaism, and the eleven disciples, the closest followers of Jesus during his public ministry, refused to accept what was overpowering in its nature and effects. For each group the resurrection of Jesus would force a major shifting of all the furniture in their lives. For the Sanhedrin, the Scriptures and the traditions of their ancestors had reached an unexpected fulfillment and must now be reinterpreted in the light of Jesus. It is all the difference between building a house and then beginning to live in it! For the disciples, Jesus' resurrection meant that the kingdom of God would not catapult them to world prestige but would make ever greater demands upon them.

In any case, Jesus' resurrection rolled away more than the stones guarding the entrance to his tomb. It flung wide the doors into the future, and no one could anticipate ahead of time what kind of life lay beyond those doors. Up till now, the Jewish leaders were able to control their individual steps and bring the ancient Scriptures to bear upon their questions and problems. By comparing and relating the ancient traditions, acceptable answers could be found. For Jesus' immediate disciples, especially the eleven who followed him closely during his ministry of preaching and healing, the future could be controlled through Jesus' miraculous power and piercing wisdom. Sitting upon thrones with Jesus, they would judge the world.

Each group was now stripped of power and control. What blocked the Jewish leaders seemed to be the enthusiasm of the Jerusalem people, praising God for what they saw happen in the healing of the crippled man. The eleven were baffled and annoyed that the first announcement of Jesus' resurrection was brought by a woman, Mary Magdalene, and by two relatively unimportant men who had already decided that their hopes about Jesus were a wild but unfortunate dream. They would go back to their former occupations. The eleven, moreover, were being sent on a mission so vague and yet so demanding that they were terrified.

In each case a true disciple of Jesus is made to realize that the first task is directed to the person of Jesus. We are to love and admire Jesus, to consecrate ourselves to his sacred person, to place more importance on prayer than on action, to realize first what it means to be a disciple of Jesus before we seek to spread the message. The eleven were certainly not being called to a contemplative existence in the desert; they were summoned to be apostles. As they went forth to the ends of the earth, their proclamation of the good news was to bear a quality of contemplative wonder and of personal devotedness for Jesus.

The Jewish leaders were not being asked to forget their traditions and Scriptures so as to contemplate Jesus, as though in Jesus alone all questions would be solved. They too, even when converted into followers of Jesus, as happened to many (Acts 6:7), would continue to draw upon their sacred Scriptures. The gospel writers would continually turn to the Hebrew Bible to understand the mystery of Jesus and to preach the message of salvation.

Both the Jewish leaders and the eleven were first required to accept, blindly out of overwhelming love, forcefully out of divine mystery, that Jesus was the Messiah, the Savior, even the very offspring of God, equal to God. Jesus would cast a new light upon all previous knowledge. How the promises would converge could not be anticipated. The future belonged to God. The disciples of Jesus must use every human means yet most of all they must realize that the love of Jesus will draw the disciples into ways and byways never known by them to exist. Jesus will make new demands, which the disciple up till now would consider impossible. Life cannot be controlled, for the secret of its inner mystery belongs to God alone.

Are we willing and able to allow the love of Jesus to cast such a bright light upon our plans for the future or upon our knowledge and information, so that we are plunged far beyond our control? Do we believe that Jesus has risen in our lives, in our hopes, in our plans, in our understanding of the Bible and theology, in our organization of Church, in our desires for our family? If Jesus has risen here at the heart of our existence, then our lives will be as transformed as we know to have happened to the eleven and to Judaism.

Prayer:

My strength and my courage reside in you, O Lord, because I do not know how to handle the wonder of your love and the transforming power of your resurrection. I praise you, Lord, for you have answered me far beyond my dreams. You have opened new gates of justice and peace.

Monday—Second Week of Easter

Acts 4:23–31. After the Christian community offered a prayer for the deliverance of Peter and John, the room shook and they were all filled with the Holy Spirit. They continued to speak God's word with confidence.

John 3:1–8. Nicodemus came to Jesus at night and was told that a person must be born again from above, through the Spirit.

When and where the Spirit comes, with what signs and consequences, cannot be determined ahead of time. "The wind blows where it will.... You do not know where it comes from or where it goes." In both Hebrew and Greek one and the same word means wind and spirit. Nor can a previous reception of the Spirit determine how it will be done the next time. In today's gospel, as again in Acts 10:44–48, the Spirit descends unexpectedly. In fact, the sudden gift of the Spirit to the unbaptized household of the Roman cohort, "religious and God-fearing," yet non-Jewish and non-Christian, took even Peter by surprise. Yet immediately Peter exclaimed: "What can stop these people who have received the Holy Spirit, even as we have, from being baptized with water?" Peter is willing to accept all the consequences of immediately baptizing pagan Romans, without first demanding the observance of the Jewish law about circumcision. Peter thus anticipated St. Paul in opening the doors of the Church to gentiles.

The convergence of many circumstances, leading up to the gift of the Holy Spirit, may also take us by surprise. Some of these details will not be holy or spiritual! In their prayer the Christian assembly refers to people who conspired in folly against the Lord and to others who "gathered in this very city against your holy servant, Jesus, 'whom you anointed.'" Jesus speaks with Nicodemus whose mind is clouded and who attempts to neutralize Jesus' highly spiritual statements with very earthly ones. Nicodemus hints to the foolishness of this talk! "How can a man be born again once he is old? Can he return to his mother's womb?" Despite such opposition, whether it be sinful or violent, or bordering on sarcasm, nonetheless, the Holy Spirit suddenly and wondrously manifests God's presence.

The gift of the Spirit shakes a person's life to its roots; it induces new birth. It overcomes all opposition, be it military, political or religious. It states positively and unmistakably: you are an entirely new person. You live a new life. Everything about you will look different. Your responses to friends, your hopes for yourself or for your family and community, your ideals, your scale of values—all these vital aspects of life will look different. Your eyes will look out with the wonder of a newly born infant. You will run in all directions like a child and find that everything brings adventure. You will be accompanied with "cures and signs and wonders to be worked in the name of Jesus."

Yet at the same time, you remain the same person that you were before. What the Spirit achieves is not a new birth but a re-birth. A person does not reenter his mother's womb. Rather an interior transformation takes place which activates hidden potential, which enlightens what was covered over with darkness (Jesus said, "I am the light!"), which sharpens what had become dull and boring (Jesus said, "I am the salt of the earth!").

This same sense of continuity is manifest in the quoting of Scripture. To explain better or to be more at peace with what is happening, the community prays in the words of ancient Scripture. It quotes Psalm 2, originally composed for the coronation of a Davidic king at Jerusalem. The Christians reach as far back as the moment of creation: "Sovereign Lord, who made heaven and earth and sea and all that is in them." God has been preparing for this moment since the dawn of creation. This eternal reach, from beginning to end of the universe, in time and space, begins to characterize the Christian prayer more and more, as we notice in such passages as Acts 14:15; 17:24; Revelation 10:6; 14:7. This outreach to creation is probably addressing the same mystery as Jesus' words to Nicodemus that a person must be reborn or re-created.

Once again, however, continuity does not mean repetition. While we remain the same person, now and into eternity, now and through each serious rebirth or conversion-experience, still we must be open to surprises. "The wind blows where it will. . . . You do not know where it comes from or where it goes." To be ready for colossal surprises and heroic transitions, the spirit will form within us that special type of "confidence" with which the Acts of the Apostles concludes today's reading. The Greek word, *'upomone,* implies an interior strength, a firm assurance, a sense of holding things together, a calm fearlessness.

Prayer:

Though problems and difficulties rise like armies in revolt, still, O Lord, I put my trust in you. With this reborn strength I will rule nations and always possess my soul. Happy will I be.

Tuesday—Second Week of Easter

Acts 4:32–37. The first Christians at Jerusalem sold their possessions and held all things in common.

John 3:7–15. Jesus spoke of a mysterious rebirth through the Spirit. He also declared that the Son of Man must be lifted up the way Moses lifted up the bronze serpent in the desert.

Today's Scriptures present so many ideas that move in different directions that we are baffled how a single unity of life and mind can be achieved. True, the early Christians at Jerusalem pooled all their resources, and there was no one in financial distress—at least for a while. Later, however, their destitution was such that Paul has to take up a collection during his travels in Greece for the sake of the Jerusalem community. Communal sharing of goods remained an ideal but was quickly abandoned as a prescribed way of life.

Other movements in the biblical readings leave us pulled in various ways and produce a strange tension within us. "No one has gone up ... except the One who came down." Yet, Jesus came down to lift us up! Once he was lifted up in glory, he returned to our lowliness. We are left on earth but attracted by Jesus towards heaven. Furthermore, to be lifted up implies glory and triumph. Yet, the image of Moses' lifting up the serpent recalls the sins of the Israelites in the desert (Num 21:4–9). When they grumbled and acted like gluttons, poisonous serpents struck among them with fiery pain and frequent death. When the Israelites looked upon a bronze or copper serpent which Moses had lifted up—and looked with repentance and honest admission of their guilt—they were cured.

The two expressions of tension may come together in an unusual way. The idealism of the early Christians draws admiration and a nostalgic desire to relive such idyllic days. How wonderful if we shared all our goods, cared for one another, were equal in wealth and poverty, and found our greatest contentment and strength in community love and God's protecting providence. Yet, doesn't it often happen that our gifts and talents, our ideals and hopes, get us into trouble and divide us one from another? We become too demanding. We insist that others follow our insights which happen to be different from their insights and talents. The artist tends to be too impractical for the administrator, the talented person becomes personally ambitious, the capable leader turns into a dictator, the scholar demands our consent before we have time to think out the question.

Peace comes, not by suppressing the gifts of the Spirit, but by humbly realizing that no one has a corner on all the gifts. Each gifted person needs all other talented people, in order to be a balanced, normal human being. Tensions then are healthy, because they prevent us from speeding in any single direction and overlooking other turns and possibilities. Tensions also remind us that gifts are given, not so much to be personally and individually activated and fulfilled, but rather to be shared in the joy and love of family. In other words, none of us, no matter how perfectly we may have fulfilled ourselves, can be saved unless our talents have been shared with others and balanced with the gifts possessed by others.

It is very difficult to allow our finest gifts to be transformed into something different than we ourselves anticipated; such a change happens when they are shared with the gifts of others. Perfect manhood and perfect womanhood do not lead to still more perfect manhood and womanhood. Rather they are intended to be blended together and produce something different: marriage and children. Or, they are called to priesthood and religious life where community life and church apostolate can shift values around and make a person's major talents to be subservient to other, seemingly lesser gifts.

A person with extraordinary mental gifts may be paralyzed so that the hidden gift of a quiet serenity may be imparted to others. A married couple may be unable to have their own children, so that they can bestow their love upon children without a home. An unimposing country pastor like John Paul I may be advanced to the papacy, in order to teach simplicity, directness and graciousness. Power then is subservient to humility.

Community then not only balances us, lest our gifts get out of hand, but it also brings extraordinary surprises into our lives. These ways of growth take place within community, because here is where the Spirit dwells.

Prayer:
The Lord indeed is king and has made the world firm, not to be moved. Yet, you, O Lord, bring stability and continuity into our lives when your Holy Spirit shakes us up, challenges us with the gifts you bestow on others and asks us to take the ultimate risk of sharing our best. Your kingdom of strength and firmness consists in family love and community sharing.

Wednesday—Second Week of Easter

Acts 5:17–26. An angel frees Peter and John from prison
and orders them to "go out now and ... preach all
about this new life" in the temple. They are again tak-
en by the temple guards, but without a show of arms
for fear of the people.

John 3:16–21. God so loved the world as to give his only
son that whoever believes in him will not die. ... He
who acts in truth comes to the light.

The Scriptures present two aspects of our salvation.
On one side we are told about world forces and even su-
per-world powers which war against one another. Peter
and John are caught in a struggle that involves the high
priest and the entire Sanhedrin besides the temple guards.
Peter and John are imprisoned. God sends angels to intervene. This same mighty struggle across the universe
breaks upon us in John's gospel about God's sending his
only son as the light of this world. Light and darkness
clash, leading to a judgment decreed for the universe.

Along with this world struggle we also glimpse the
insignificant ways of everyday life and the normal routine
of ordinary people. After being freed by an angel, Peter
and John are again in the temple courtyard, preaching to
an enthusiastic group of people. They are almost ignoring
their marvelous deliverance, acting as though nothing
had taken place, whether it be their imprisonment by the
powerful forces of Judaism or their wondrous deliverance
by an angel. And when the police force intervenes, they
must do so "without any show of force for fear of being
stoned by the crowd." Somehow or other, these ordinary
people without any military arms except the stones on
the ground by which they can annoy the police, bring the
police to peaceful submission. Likewise, in John's gospel,

Jesus seemingly asks for nothing other than sincerity, to act "in truth," and to live in the light of his presence.

The deep intuitive faith of people at large then turns out to be the stable ingredient of religion. Their matter-of-fact response, their enthusiasm, their spontaneous rallying around defenseless Peter and John, their ability to call everything and everyone by their right name, their continuing loyalty, their confidence in Jesus' presence in their midst, their spirit of hope in the goodness of God's creation—here is where the difference is made between success or failure in accomplishing God's will for our salvation.

Any number of questions are put to us by these ordinary people. Do we attempt to control everything by human ingenuity? Do we have a false kind of security, that makes us so deadly serious about having everything in its proper place? Does this somber, rational grip upon life eat away at our spontaneous joy and exuberant faith in life? Are we afraid to take any chances, because we really do not have that much trust in God or in one another? Do we make everything and everyone gravitate around ourselves, selfishly for our own benefit—on the pretext that we thus keep everything "very good"? Are we free and unstudied in witnessing to our faith in Jesus? Does our whole way of life manifest the "light" which Jesus' presence radiates in our midst? Or do we tend to be depressed and melancholy? Are we fearful and suspicious?

Our faith in the supernatural keeps us sensitively aware that mighty forces of goodness and evil are clashing roundabout us—whether these be angels and devils or economic and military forces, faith in God or militant atheism, enthusiastic belief in Jesus as Savior or passive indifference. Yet, our response to these titanic clashes does not, or at least should not, turn out to be on the human level of control, fear, suspicion and rational human management. While all these emotions and reactions have a place, they should not be our basic attitude. Beneath all these human forces and earthly realities there ought to lie our strong faith in Jesus as our light, our way, our warmth.

Jesus, therefore, not only begets life by his intimate love, but Jesus also nourishes that life by his family love. His presence is as clear as the light of the sun, surrounding us on every side. And yet like the sunlight, Jesus too evades our understanding and can never be controlled. Gently the warm light of Jesus coaxes us to grow in love and trust. It endorses a warm enthusiasm for life, trust in others, quickness to rally around whatever is good, noble and worthy of faith (Phil 4:8).

Prayer:

Lord, your angel encamps around us, so that no evil force can overcome us, whether accidental or calculated. Whenever I turn to you and seek you, you are already there, drawing me to yourself. Yes, I affirm the words of the psalmist: "Taste and see how good the Lord is. Happy the one who takes refuge in him."

Thursday—Second Week of Easter

Acts 5:27–33. Peter and John are again before the highest
court of the land, the Sanhedrin. They fearlessly declare: "Better for us to obey God than human authority." Those rejected by men and women, God raised
from the dead. "We testify to this and so does the Holy
Spirit whom God gives to those who obey."

John 3:31–36. Jesus speaks of what he sees from above,
where the Father has given all things to the Son. Whoever believes in the Son, has the Spirit bestowed without measure.

It is always difficult to distinguish internal strength
from stubborn manipulation of others. How do we know
that our convictions are from God and must be obeyed at
all costs, so that we set our face against the highest authorities and clearly enunciate that it is better to obey
God than human authority? Very few if any of us have
had immediate revelations from God. How then do we
know that our convictions are from God?

To follow Jesus and thus to receive our strength and
decisions from Jesus presumes that like Jesus we walk
after him through suffering and death, even through hu-
miliations which might seem worse than death. Jesus was
hung from a tree, the most despicable and painful of
deaths. All of us, like the apostles, must go through experiences similar to death, where we have risked everything
for the sake of Jesus. The experience may have come
about because of our love for others, our willingness to
forgive and begin life all over again with them, our loss of
personal opportunities and individual security for the
sake of others whose sickness or weakness makes great
demands upon us.

A very difficult aspect of following Jesus looms before us in the call to humility. We all admire this virtue in others. Yet, we do not know when our response will be as honorable as the humble Jesus or as dishonorable as Peter in denying Jesus before some servants and their friends. A false humility fears to do anything, lest it do something to provoke pride! Refusing all responsibility, a "humble" person escapes any judgment from others. As difficult as it may be, not only to practice the virtue but even to know what it is, humble we must be if we are to follow Jesus. Humility may be the realization that all of us have the same temptations and inclinations, repeatedly throughout our life; that we have all fallen short of our ideals and that we have contributed to the sorrow of others.

Another norm for deciding if we are following Jesus in his humility is given to us in the words of Scripture: we testify to this and so does the Holy Spirit. The Holy Spirit becomes vibrant in our hearts through long periods of prayer, week by week, even day by day. We need those stretches of time during which distractions and preoccupations gradually fade away and God's presence surrounds us forcefully yet quietly like sunlight. We also hear the testimony of the Holy Spirit by checking out our ideas and responses with good advisors. We all need someone from whom we hear the honest, plain truth. This interaction with the Holy Spirit in a spiritual director or advisor will keep our quiet hours of prayer from simply a task of self-introspection. Prayer and spiritual guidance are genuine, if they not only impart peace but if they also make demands upon us to grow and develop beyond our narrowness.

Another test that we can administer to ourselves in order to see if we are guided by the Holy Spirit, is pointed out in Peter's reference to the "God of our ancestors."

Do I continuously read the Bible, so that I form a family of life and response with it? It is necessary to read on, page by page, so as to acquire an integral, whole spirituality. If we pick and choose, we may simply reenforce our own idiosyncrasies and stubborness. But if we take whatever the page offers, we will touch down on all bases of a fully human spiritual life.

This same norm of forming one family with one's ancestors in the faith also asks us to be true to our traditions. We must interact with earlier beliefs and devotions, so that our present position will seem to be a flowering of the seed that was planted in the past. Just as Jesus came forth from the Father, lived obediently to his will even unto death, and returned to the Father, we too must live and think within a similar cycle of life. Then our testimony, like Jesus', will witness to what we have seen and heard.

Prayer:

Lord God, you judge whether we are following your holy will or our own stubborn way by our concern for the poor and brokenhearted. You are close to them and hear their cry. You deliver them from distress. Keep me, Lord, at their side that I may taste and see your goodness.

Friday—Second Week of Easter

Acts 5:34–42. Jesus is compared with several false messiahs. It was stated in the Sanhedrin: if this work is of human origin, it will destroy itself, but if it is of God, no one can resist it successfully. The apostles counted it a joy to suffer in the name of Jesus.

John 6:1–15. Miracle of loaves and fishes. Jesus fled to the mountain alone when the people proclaimed him the prophet and wanted to make him king.

We are asked to examine our motives for following Jesus and our norms for judging other institutions. Personal advancement and pleasure are ruled out by the scriptural readings. When the people proclaim Jesus to be the prophet, anticipated by Moses in Deuteronomy 18:9–22, Jesus is uneasy. If he has come to fulfill the hopes and prophecies of his ancestors, why, we ask, does Jesus react this negatively when the people see the accomplishment of Scripture in him?

The false motivation consisted in this, the people wanted to make Jesus their king, in order to secure the continuous presence of Jesus' miraculous powers in their midst. What Jesus decided was good on a single occasion, the people wanted to turn into an everyday possibility. The people's action in itself was good; the reason for Jesus' displeasure must be found in the people's motivation.

In the first reading from the Acts of the Apostles, we are told that various messiahs had arisen and good people had been confused and misled. One of the Jewish leaders in the Sanhedrin then remarked: if a work is of human origin, it will destroy itself; if it is of God, no one can stop it. To fight it is to fight against God. Even so, the apostles are not fully exonorated. The Sanhedrin decides to flog the apostles before releasing them. At this the apostles rejoiced at the opportunity to suffer for the name of Jesus. They continued to preach in Jesus' name.

We are not to follow Jesus for selfish motives, for our own advancement, for our political ambition, even for our security and protection. These motives are not necessarily evil. We must be concerned about ourselves. Otherwise, we may recklessly throw our life and its opportunities to the wind, wear ourselves out uselessly or too quickly, lose the normal kind of health necessary for peace of mind, and eventually give up! Advancement of a good cause very often results in the advancement of ourselves. Good work usually draws the spotlight to the one who achieves it, and that person is asked to undertake more difficult and more important tasks. And so we touch upon the force of ambition, hope and growth. Somehow or other, even our security depends upon our ability to grow and develop to live with the times and adapt to new situations.

Sooner or later, however, these motives become insufficient for the challenge before us. For the sake of our family and community, in order to honor commitments and promises, in the face of serious threats to our faith in God and in the Church—we are forced to seek strength and guidance from the deepest part of ourselves. It is no longer a question of careers, work, security and good deeds. Now we are faced with the heroic decision of deciding to be true to our conscience before extraordinary demands. We come right up against a case of life or death.

In one way or another, our deepest motivation will be tested. Our trust in God's goodness will be stretched to the breaking point. Our loyalty to our family or community or church will seem almost self-destructive, so much will be expected of us. We too like the apostles will suffer from the scourge and flogging. Yet through the presence of the Holy Spirit in our heart and in our community, we too like the apostles will rejoice that we have been chosen to suffer for the name of Jesus.

Our response to others in the midst of their suffering ought to be guided by convictions of faith. In other words, at times we strengthen others by our convictions that their cause is just, their risk is necessary, their conscience comes before all else. They are able to suffer—and to rejoice in their suffering—for the name of Jesus. Sometimes, therefore, we ought not to alleviate suffering but help a person to face it with faith.

Finally, we have the assurance—if a work is of God, it cannot be destroyed. To fight it is to fight against God. Therefore, no suffering is wasted energy.

And as we look about us at people who have survived heroic tests of endurance or at institutions that have continued to exist over the centuries, we ought to be convinced that such expressions are godly. Otherwise, they would have died a long time ago. There are many such institutions which deserve much more respect than we often give them. They must have proven not only that they are from God but also that their motivation is divinely inspired.

Thus we continue to preach the good news of Jesus the Messiah.

Prayer:

Lord, you are my light and my salvation. Whom should I fear? Nothing can separate me from your love, neither trial nor distress, nor persecution, nor hunger, neither death nor life. In all such moments I gaze upon your loveliness, O Lord.

Saturday—Second Week of Easter

Acts 6:1–7. The choice of seven deacons for the Greek-speaking Christians; the conversion of many Jewish priests to the Christian community.

John 6:16–21. During a storm at sea Jesus walks on the water toward the boat with the disciples who suddenly find themselves at shore.

The gospel presents two moments in our lives: one in which we move ahead without Jesus and find ourselves engulfed with hostile waves ready to destroy us; another in which Jesus is suddenly with us and we find ourselves at our destination. Putting the two scriptural passages together, we see a sudden, miraculous change in the gospel. In Acts, on the contrary, the apostles heal a major division in the ranks by human compromise and common sense. The Greek-speaking community of believers find that their widows are being neglected by the Church, out of favoritism for those native born in the Holy Land and speaking Hebrew. The Twelve ask the community to seek out seven men, deeply spiritual and prudent, to oversee the care of the Greek-speaking widows.

Normally, we are expected to make good use of our intelligence and common sense. This procedure means, first of all, that we are not overly discouraged and then give up, because of favoritism and jealousy in the church. The right response ought not to be anger or rejection. The apostles, moreover, did not move in like petty dictators and quickly rectify the situation. While they made a prudent decision, still they left the implementation of it to the community. The Twelve felt that they should not neglect their duty of preaching and teaching. They asked the Greek-speaking community to elect their representatives, seven deacons, known for their piety and prudence.

They were then publicly ordained by the laying on of hands.

Yet, we ought not to rule out the possibility even of miraculous intervention on God's part. God can, and at times does step in and immediately change the situation from one of desperation to one of new life. In the gospel the disciples immediately found themselves aground on the shore; their fears of drowning at sea or at least of serious danger were quickly wiped away. They had not even prayed for such a miracle. When the possibility became real and Jesus appeared walking on the water, they were naturally frightened.

Miracles then can quickly remove all fear and danger, yet their very possibility induces a new kind of fear! If God can intervene wondrously in our daily lives, then we have lost control. We do not know exactly what God will do. Miracles are not discussed and voted on; they simply happen! Belief in miracles presumes an attitude which surrenders the ultimate decision of life to God. It is a state of mind that does not demand complete control. It is willing to live that very risky existence—that adventure of faith—whereby God can step in at crucial moments and shift gears for us. Ultimately, it means a readiness to die any time. A step back from death, it means an openness to radical changes.

These changes can seem so fearful that we could become totally distraught at the thought of it. We should note that such changes are not necessarily planned by the disciples. For instance, in the gospel, the winds blew up a storm unexpectedly, in the midst of the night, while the disciples had rowed three or four miles from the shore. We are not speaking of changes we plan. Rather, they are God's secret which suddenly bursts upon us. Therefore, a healthy continuity remains in our lives. Yet, within its step-by-step progress God at times picks us up and launches us like a rocket into the future.

Continuity, therefore, is necessary. And when problems arise, our first recourse ought to be humanly thought out. First, we remain with our community or family. We do not stomp out because of jealousy and favoritism, even if these latter faults are among the surest signs of failure as disciples of Jesus. Nor do we respond so angrily that a shouting match breaks out! In the Acts of the Apostles we are amazed at the quiet style of the Twelve. Along with prudence and common sense, they have recourse to prayer. Once these human means have been put to good service, they publicly, solemnly and religiously endorse the results. They impose hands upon the heads of the seven deacons before the entire community at prayer. Here is the origin of the sacred order of deacons.

It was then this combination of human precaution and supernatural prayer, of earlier sin and restrained patience, of clear decision and delegation of authority, of human politics and divine endorsement, it was all of these moments wrapped into a single process that made the early Church develop and spread. Today's liturgical account ends with a statement that many Jewish priests embraced the faith.

Prayer:

Lord, in the midst of our anxieties and difficulties, when our patience and ideals are strained to the breaking point, we turn to you and place our trust in you. You love justice and right; you will not allow prejudice and oppression to destroy us. Your eyes are upon those who fear you and hope for your kindness.

Monday—Third Week of Easter

Acts 6:8–15. Stephen, one of the new deacons, is brought before the Sanhedrin on false charges. His face seems that of an angel.

John 6:22–29. The crowds looked for Jesus, not because they had seen a sign of God's mysterious power but because they had eaten their fill of perishable food.

The key word here is "look"! When the members of the Sanhedrin looked on the face of Stephen it "seemed like that of an angel." Jesus tells the crowd: "You are not looking for me because you have seen signs but because you have eaten your fill of the loaves."

Each of us looks outward in many different ways: with wide interest or with narrow bias, with a large heart open to goodness everywhere or with a narrow focus limited to personal concerns, with faith that accepts even miracles or with pessimism that sees only the worst, with wonder that peers beneath the surface to teeming possibilities or with a dull shrug of the shoulders that hardly pays attention to miracles! Somehow or other, our present world and all the more surely our future existence turn into what we see—at least so far as our own personal life is concerned.

A saint like Stephen, ordained to care for the poor and for neglected widows, was endowed by God with such a large heart that he overlooked trivia and did not allow himself to be caught on the sticky paper of petty worries. Instead of such narrow-mindedness, he reached out to the needs of the helpless. Yet he was dragged before the court for acting against the customs of the people. Important, intelligent people were willing to argue about customs when the poor were going hungry. The members of the Sanhedrin looked at a saint and turned him into a sinner. They saw the face of an angel and twisted it into that of a devil.

When Jesus fed the hungry in the wilderness, they were concerned only about stuffing food between their teeth. They did not ask about the goodness and generosity of God who cares for them; they did not inquire about their ways of sharing with others and so of imitating the goodness of Jesus. They did not stop to listen to the words of Jesus, ponder them prayerfully and ask for their implications in their daily lives. They simply wanted more food.

Eventually, John's gospel links this miraculous multiplication of bread and fish with the Eucharist—Jesus' very own body and blood given for the life of the world.

The Eucharist enables us to look with the eyes of Jesus and to see so much more than we ever thought to exist round about us. We look at strangers and see them as our brothers and sisters. We look at people whom we consider hopeless, intransigent and incommunicable, and find a bond of concern and interests about which to speak with them. Devils somehow turn into saints! Those who seemed lost have been found!

Every person and every event become a sign. They are like the tip of an iceberg, which conceals far more than it reveals, which alerts us to a mystery of power beyond our imagination. It asks us to look long and to study with open minds. We accept the invitation to walk into a wonderful way of life with goodness and hope beyond our imagination. We look with our feelings and intuitions, with our hopes and dreams. We see what will take an eternity to explore in all its possibilities. In fact, our eternity will consist at least partially of the joyful amazement of learning ever anew all the goodness which existed in people whose hands we shook during earthly life yet whose heart we never touched.

God has set his seal on Jesus and on all the mysteries which Jesus reveals. To look as Jesus looks, to look at something very earthly and to recognize a divine mystery, means that we are sealing our lives in a bond of love that will last forever. To look in this way, then, does not only mean that we see wonders but also that our own selves are inextricably linked with that wonder for all eternity. The Eucharist then is the food of eternal life.

Prayer:

Lord, help me so that I choose your way of truth. Then I will look with your eyes, see wondrous deeds, intuit undreamed of possibilities, and find great delight. Happy will I be. My eyes will be cleansed to see mysteries. The goodness which I see, O Lord, will purify me. I will then hear the words of your psalmist and realize how true they are: Happy are those of blameless life. The goodness which I shall then see will attract me so strongly, that I will know no other law but the demands of such hopes.

Tuesday—Third Week of Easter
Acts 7:51–8:1. The martyrdom of Stephen
John 6:30–35. Jesus is the bread come down from heaven. No one who comes to Jesus will hunger and thirst any more.

In presenting the *Acta* of the martyrdom of St. Stephen, Luke the author carefully models the death scene of Stephen upon Jesus' death on the cross. Both, accused of blasphemy, are condemned to death by the Sanhedrin. Each sees a vision of someone at the right hand of God, coming on the clouds—a reference to Daniel's vision in describing the vindication of the martyr saints of Old Testament times (Dan 7:9–14). Each asks God to receive the spirit and each prays for the forgiveness of the executioners (See Luke 22–23).

Another kind of comparison occurs in John's gospel, Chapter 6. Jesus and Moses stand side by side. While each announces bread from heaven, the manna promised by Moses perished by the next day and stopped appearing once the Israelites crossed the Jordan and settled in the promised land (Josh 5:12). The bread which Jesus provides brings eternal life. It slakes all thirst and satisfies every hunger. Jesus alone offers life which will never end.

Yet, the Acts of the Apostles seems at first to contradict this promise of life. Jesus himself died on the cross, and Stephen becomes the proto-martyr of Christianity. Yet, when death is modeled upon that of Jesus, we know that the highest honor has been bestowed upon a person. Such a death turns into a moment of triumph and glory! The last moments of Stephen, however, seemed anything but glorious and joyful. A pall of sorrow must have descended upon the small Christian community. Luke adds at once, at the beginning of the next chapter of *Acts:*

"That day saw the beginning of a great persecution of the church in Jerusalem. All except the apostles scattered throughout the countryside of Judea and Samaria. . . . After that, Saul began to harass the Church."

Some members of the Church must have experienced a profound sense of pain and frustration; they must have been angry at themselves. It was their complaints about the way their widows were being neglected that led to the appointment of the first seven deacons; Stephen was among them. Given this position of authority and visibility within the small Christian community and almost at once because of his ability to draw upon the ancient Scriptures and to speak eloquently, Stephen became the lightning rod that attracted the electricity in the air. It struck him violently and destructively.

Even someone as well meaning as Saul of Tarsus approved of the action against Stephen. As we read in *Acts:* "Saul, for his part, concurred in the act of killing." Pain and frustration, anger and confusion—all these emotions surrounded the martyrdom of Stephen.

Stephen himself responded with peace—he was "filled with the Holy Spirit." Even though he was dragged outside the city and a volcano was erupting around him, he prayed that Jesus whom he had seen at God's right hand would now come to receive him into that heavenly peace. At once Stephen shared that peace with everyone about him. He prayed that his executioners be forgiven.

In other words, Stephen did not answer anger with anger, nor did he match frustration with frustration. He rose above the gloom and violence by the strength which he absorbed from Jesus. This calm self-possession enabled Stephen to reason forcefully with those who summoned him to the court of the Sanhedrin. It enabled him to recognize God's providence and design where everyone else was caught in regrets, anger, frustration and violence. Where base or unworthy human emotions cut through the lives of people, Stephen remained in possession of himself because he had surrendered that possession to the Lord Jesus.

We too are called to respond with faith. We are expected to remain at peace, even though violence explodes round about us. We do not let others call the shots nor play the tune to which we must dance.

We have a source of strength to survive any desert. From Jesus we receive the food and drink for our soul so that we do not faint from thirst or hunger. Jesus provides this nourishment, like Moses, to us his people as we tramp through the desert. In such a dry stretch of wasteland, we walk more from willpower and desires than from any natural energy. We live by our hopes. We rise above the environment. Our faith preserves us at our best, because we have already surrendered ourselves to Jesus.

We pray: "Lord Jesus, receive my spirit."

Prayer:

Into your hands, O Lord, I entrust my spirit. To you I confide my hopes. In you I seek my strength. Let your face shine upon me and then I will experience the attraction of your love and share that peaceful joy with all others.

Wednesday—Third Week of Easter

Acts 8:1–8. Persecution broke out after the martyrdom of Stephen; miracles and conversions bring rejoicing in the countryside, especially among the Samaritans.

John 6:35–40. Jesus attracts everyone whom the Father has given to him. He sustains them as their life-giving bread, will reject no one and raises them up on the last day.

Jerusalem, which had been a special object of Jesus' ministry, violently rejects his disciples; the countryside, particularly Samaria, listens carefully to the word, possesses the faith to accept miracles, and converts to the Lord. Jerusalem, the sophisticated city with its religious schools and centuries old traditions, with its large number of religious leaders and educational movements, never gives Jesus or his disciples a fair chance to explain themselves; while Samaria, neglected, oppressed, half-learned and half-ignorant, fearful and closed toward mass movements yet open and spontaneous toward affection and sincerity, listens to the disciples, experiences miracles of body and mind, and responds with joy and ecstatic wonder.

The comparison of Jerusalem with Samaria alerts us to the advantages and disadvantages of strong, continuous intellectual preparation for the gospel. No doubt, Jerusalem became the source of strength and continuity for the religion of Moses. Humanly speaking, the religion of Israel would have disappeared like the religion of the Philistines or Moabites, if Jerusalem had collapsed and disappeared. At Jerusalem the sacred tradition was preserved, and at crucial times adapted and revised in a new written form. Jerusalem was also the center for the great rabbinical schools and for the central governing body of

Judaism. Yet, it was Jerusalem which violently rejected Jesus and his first disciples.

Samaria, the step-child of Mosaic religion, partially correct and partially wrong in religious beliefs and practices, hostile toward outsiders yet warm and open once a person manifested sincerity and personal warmth, accepted the faith. Not all the Samaritans, but a good number of them converted. It is possible that part of their enthusiasm or at least their protection of Jesus' disciples stemmed from the Samaritan hostility toward Jerusalem. If Jerusalem rejected the disciples, then the Samaritans would naturally be inclined to accept them!

There was a direct simplicity about the Samaritans. As a result, hidden resources could quickly come to the surface. New possibilities would be acted upon. They were not afraid of sophisticated criticism leveled at the Samaritan naiveté.

All of us possess hidden resources and untapped potential. Here is where we are liable to be fearful. Here is where we can easily make mistakes. Here is also where genius is born, wonderful new insights leap forth, extraordinary turns of fortune take place. We know people who are sleepers. We suspected their talents yet were never sure. They seemed hesitant; they remained behind the others; they were silent. Then suddenly, the flower blooms and all the potential goodness of the person comes to the surface.

Jesus may look upon us as people too sophisticated for our own good. Because we know religion so well—maybe because we are leaders, ministers, priests and bishops—we can make religion a substitute for religious fervor. We are the Jerusalem of the Acts of the Apostles: possessing the great heritage and yet denying its fulfillment.

Yet, the disciples of Jesus go out to the countryside, to Samaria. Jesus' word reaches our hidden talents. All of a sudden, the "devil" which has kept us silent, fearful, unable to speak, or willing to speak only in strange, devious ways, is driven out of us. We are cured! "The rejoicing in that town rose to fever pitch."

Jesus too said: all that the Father gives me shall come to me. I shall lose nothing of what he has given me. I shall raise it up on the last day. We can anticipate the day of resurrection. We can have everlasting life now—if we look to the Son, Our Lord Jesus Christ. We allow our hopes and talents to be touched by Jesus' warmth. We are willing to take the full consequences of our new way of life, with its enthusiasm and achievement.

Prayer:

Let all the earth cry out to God with joy. What was dried up and barren, becomes the source of life and tremendous deeds. By our surrendering in faith, Lord Jesus, people can come and see your wonders in our lives.

Thursday—Third Week of Easter

Acts 8:26–40. The deacon Philip meets the Ethiopian
treasurer to the royal court and explains Isaiah 53 in
terms of Jesus. He then baptizes the Ethiopian.

John 6:44–51. No one comes to me, Jesus said, unless the
Father draws that person. And whoever eats the bread
come down from heaven, lives forever. Jesus' flesh is
for the life of the world.

The heavenly Father was already drawing the Ethiopian eunuch and royal treasurer to faith. This foreigner
was already a "God-fearer," the term given for gentiles
who believed in Yahweh, the God of Israel, and followed
many of the prescriptions of the Torah, but not all of
them, especially those which would alienate the foreigner
from his own family and country. Yahweh, moreover,
was attracting the Ethiopian ever more deeply into the
religion of Israel through his reading of the prophet Isaiah and the Suffering Servant Songs.

God also directed the deacon Philip to head south
along the same route taken by the Ethiopian. In many
ways then God's plans were converging upon the Ethiopian. Yet, something was still lacking and the Ethiopian
felt helpless. "Do you really grasp what you are reading?" "How can I unless someone explains it to me?"
Philip then explained the meaning of the Suffering Servant Song:

> Like a sheep he was led to the slaughter,
>   like a lamb before its shearer he was
>   silent . . .
> Who will ever speak of his posterity?

After Philip re-read the passage in terms of Jesus and contemplated with the Ethiopian the profound sense of the passage through Jesus' death on the cross, the God-fearer asked to be baptized and Philip at once admitted him to the church.

We observe here the steps of conversion, not only from sin to grace, nor simply from an outsider to membership within the church, but also from an opportunity of grace to its full realization.

First, we must have confidence that God is always drawing us closer to Jesus. In each moment of our lives God is summoning us from hate or displeasure to love or joy, from fear to peace, from isolation to companionship, from sin to grace, from being "good" to being "much better." We must have the same faith in others that they too are being attracted by God to a more fervent way of life and to a holier attitude. Like the Ethiopian we must be a "God-fearer," awesome and in wonder at what God is doing with ourselves and our lives. Like this foreigner, we should go regularly to community prayer and church worship, as he did to the Jerusalem temple.

This pilgrimage to the temple or church not only means a physical journey but also a spiritual walk along the pages of the Bible. The Ethiopian was reading from Isaiah Chapter 53. It is important to note that he was reading a passage and even delaying over it, despite the fact that he did not understand what the words were saying to him. He did not simply hurry onward to something within the reach of his understanding and control! He waited for the Lord to speak.

Still another pilgrimage must be made, this time by the church toward those who are being attracted by the heavenly Father. Deacon Philip was told to "head south . . . catch up with that carriage . . . [and inquire] 'Do you really grasp what you are reading?' " There must be a missionary drive within the church, with gentle initiative, asking "Do you really grasp?" The Church must also be driven by a longing to see Jesus everywhere or to believe that all good desires, even those in Scripture, are leading to "the good news of Jesus." Jesus absorbs and fulfills every good desire and strong hope.

When all of these pilgrimages come together, a person is ready to be received within the Church. The Ethiopian asked for baptism, the door to the Church. This door, however, swings back and forth. It leads the Ethiopian into the Church but it also invites him to go forth as an apostle of the good news. Deacon Philip disappears and the foreigner continues on his journey home to bring the good news to his own country.

Through the Church the Ethiopian not only receives baptism and new life in Jesus but also the bread or nourishment to sustain that life strong and vigorous. The gospel tells us:

> I myself an the living bread
> come down from heaven.
> If anyone eats this bread
> that one shall live forever.

Yet, this eucharistic nourishment also leads to death. It brings a participation in the death of Jesus. "This bread that I will give is my flesh, for the life of the world." This flesh or body of Jesus silently suffered death, as announced in Isaiah Chapter 53. Yet, in death there is a door to new life beyond human imagination. For this reason baptism too is compared to death, a sharing in the death of Jesus (Rom 6:3).

Life comes in extraordinary ways. The Ethiopian

treasurer is called a "eunuch." The word may not have to be taken literally as someone unable to beget children. At this time it had acquired a more general sense of a court official; in ancient days, these men had to be eunuchs in the physical sense of the term. Yet, in the passage we see several persons, all seemingly without offspring and without a future. The suffering servant gives rise to the question in Isaiah: "Who will ever speak of his posterity, for he is deprived of his life on earth?" Jesus died, a total failure from all appearances. The Ethiopian may have been deprived of descendants. Through Jesus' resurrection life and offspring come in mysterious ways.

Prayer:

Lord, we cry out to you joyfully. You have changed our loneliness and sterility into joy and life, for ourselves and for a family beyond our human power to beget. Through baptism into the Church, we find this family; in eternity we enjoy its companionship. I appealed to you, O Lord, and you did not refuse me your kindness.

Friday—Third Week of Easter

Acts 8:26–40. First account of the conversion of Paul,
emphasizing his role toward the evangelization of the
gentiles and his call to suffer for the gospel.

John 6:52–59. Unless you eat the flesh and drink the
blood of the Son of Man, you do not have life; the one
who does has life eternal.

Paul's conversion is presented for the first of three
times in the Acts of the Apostles. Here it highlights the
movement of the church beyond Judaism to the gentile
world. This account is preceded in Acts by the story of
the Ethiopian eunuch who was baptized by deacon Philip
and then proceeded to bring the gospel to his own country. It is followed, again in Acts, by the conversion of the
Roman centurion Cornelius. Both the Ethiopian and
Cornelius were baptized without going through the full
procedures of first becoming a Jew by circumcision and
by accepting stringent dietary laws. The conversion of
these foreigners shared an important feature with Paul's
conversion. Each took place because of special, almost
miraculous intervention by God.

The Ethiopian was drawn to Christianity through
his reading about the Suffering Servant in Isaiah Chapter
53. Philip explains the passage in terms of Jesus' death
and resurrection. Now in Paul's case these same passages
from Isaiah about the Suffering Servant describe the vocation of this new apostle. Jesus, in appearing to Ananias
and instructing him to baptize Paul, draws ideas and
phrases from the Servant Songs and applies them to Paul.
Conversion, therefore, meant a sharing in the silent death
and the glorious resurrection of Jesus—and in that order,
first death, then new life.

Up till now Paul had been persecuting the Church,

in Jerusalem and now (he had thought) in Damascus. His conversion, however, would bring an entirely new type of suffering to the small group of disciples. In becoming an apostle to the gentiles, Paul insisted that it was not necessary to be circumcised nor to follow Mosaic laws like those for food and drink, in order to be a follower of Jesus. This action on Paul's part split the Church right down the center. The controversy comes to the surface in Paul's Epistle to the Galatians and in a later chapter in Acts. Paul, therefore, was considered a traitor by his own Jewish family and coreligionists, and he was to be isolated and calumniated even by his Christian community. When Jesus announced to Ananias that Paul "will have to suffer for my name," he was referring not just to Paul's eventual martyrdom in Rome but even more to a life of martyrdom within his own Church! In such a situation, the Church itself suffered, once again from Paul, but in a much different way than when he dragged Christians off to prison in Jerusalem for confessing the name of Jesus.

Family and Church mean the greatest joy but the words also spell the most intense pain. Such was the case for Paul and for Jesus. Against this background of family life and death, of family joy and pain, we can reread Jesus' words. ". . . eat the flesh of the Son of Man and drink his blood. . . . I will raise up on the last day . . . who feeds on my flesh and drinks my blood remains in me and I in that person . . . will have life because of me." The eucharistic bread and wine—the body and blood of Jesus— is closely associated with Jesus death, with "my body broken for you . . . my blood which will be shed for you" (Luke 22:19–20).

Because Jesus was plunged so thoroughly into the Jewish race (born of Abraham and of the family of David, as we learn from his genealogy in Matthew 1:1–17 and Luke 3:23–38), a struggle unto death ensued. Neither he nor his Jewish community could ignore one another. They were in it together like members of a family. Even after Jesus was handed over to the Romans by the high court of the Sanhedrin and executed, his disciples continued to live and worship as Jews. The Eucharist was celebrated privately at home. The love-hate relationship of every family existed here. The ones who brought the greatest joy inflicted the most intense pain! And on one another!

Wherever then we bring the good news of Jesus and the family love of the Eucharist, we are also instruments of suffering. Our lives are intertwined as closely as flesh and blood. Blood brings the strength and vigor for flesh to suffer crucifixion. Flesh keeps the blood circulating within a single body where we are all united.

Once Paul was converted, both he and the Church took the consequences. Each would suffer the effect of the other's gifts, insights and apostolate. And as each one is strengthened further by Jesus' eucharistic bread come down from heaven, each will be clearer in insights, more forceful in demands and expectations, even more impatient at the slow or indifferent reaction of others. This process of life, into death, for a new and greater life is the story of Jesus, Paul and each of us.

Prayer:

Lord, you send us to the whole world to announce your Good News. We are exhilarated when we witness people of all nations glorifying you as their Savior. Help us to remain within the steady bond of your love within community; let our fidelity endure forever, like yours, even at the cost of the suffering which we inflict upon one another.

Saturday—Third Week of Easter

Acts 9:31–42. After the death of Stephen and the initial
persecution at that time, the Church enjoys a new
peace. Miracles take place and many converts join the
church. Dorcas is raised back to life by Peter.

John 6:60–69. Jesus alone has words of eternal life, yet
these are "hard to endure," many say.

Throughout the Easter season we are being offered
an opportunity to rise to new life. Jesus is speaking, to
summon what seems dead within us and to make this
dead part of ourselves the source of an entirely new existence. At the same time, despite this radical transition
within ourselves, we continue to be the same person who
existed before the marvelous change happened. The lady
whom Peter called back to life was the same Dorcas
whose "good deeds and acts of charity" had established a
family bond with many of the poor and oppressed, particularly with the widows in the city of Joppa.

Suppose that I am called on an urgent request, without knowing the exact reason. Upon arrival, I am told
that a dead person was laid out for a final farewell before
burial. I am expected to bring that person back to life! At
that moment, I am surrounded with the family and
friends, with all the many dependents who have been assisted by the dead person. They all look to me to do
something—and that "something" amounts to bringing a
dead person back to life! What would I do?

Before I answer, however, I have the peace of mind
to meditate with the group on the gospel of St. John. God
says to me, as once in the first composition of the gospel:

This sort of talk is hard to endure!
His disciples were murmuring in protest.

It is the spirit that gives life;
   the flesh is useless,
The words I spoke to you
   are spirit and life.
Lord, to whom shall we go?
You have the words of eternal life.

These sentences from the gospel of St. John capture the many different feelings as I stand before a dead person with the request to bring this loved one back to life. Some say—myself—that it is "talk hard to endure." I feel myself murmuring in protest: why ask me? why embarrass me? I am a faithful believer, but I am no idiot, nor vain presumer, nor wild dreamer! Why pick on me?

I decide to follow Peter's example and to kneel in prayer. Whenever I pray, is it with the faith that God can work miracles, if he wills? Do I accept that God can achieve what seems impossible for flesh, for weak human nature? "It is the spirit that gives life; the flesh is useless."

God may never test my faith to the extent of calling me to the bedside of a dead person and of being asked to bring that dear one back to life. Yet, one way or another, God will test my faith. Not every day, but at crucial moments, I will be asked to do what I would consider impossible. At least, I would respond to God that his requests are unreasonable, over-demanding and therefore not binding upon my conscience.

Very few of us are called into the mission of the apostle Peter. On his numerous journeys he was *frequently* placed in a position of working miracles. God does not ask the ordinary person (that is, you and me) to be ready for miracles each day of our life, or say, once a week or even once a month! God does not make each day an act of heroic virtue, summoning strength which I never knew to exist within myself and being forced to live in the power of the Holy Spirit. "It is the spirit that gives life; the flesh is useless."

All of us, nonetheless, are summoned occasionally— and these are key moments of our existence—to work miracles. The wonder may not be as public and as startling as bringing a dead person back to life; it may be even more exacting in all its consequences. God may suddenly ask me to forgive another person (with whom I have not been speaking for years), to be silent and no longer make an issue out of an unpleasant situation, to accept a new friend or relative or member within my family, to accept the loss of a friend or relative or family member, to live silently with a physical ailment or even with an emotional disability, without complaint or even a whispering reference. Such heroic moments come occasionally. We think that God is asking the impossible. And we read in John's gospel: "It is the spirit that gives life; the flesh is useless."

Prayer:

Lord, what return can I make to you for all that you have given to me? I will take the cup of salvation, the chalice of your suffering, and drink of your precious blood. I will absorb your strength and your spirit. Then nothing will be impossible that you ask of me.

Monday—Fourth Week of Easter

Acts 11:1–18. Gentiles at Caesarea receive the Holy Spirit, before they are baptized and even before they are instructed in the Jewish law. Therefore, Peter could not refuse them baptism.

John 10:1–10. Jesus is the Good Shepherd who knows his sheep by name; he is also the gate to the safety of the sheepfold and to the nourishment of the outside pasture.

John 10:11–18* Jesus, the Good Shepherd, lays down his life for his sheep and so is loved by the Father.

The gift of the Holy Spirit is extremely personal, reaching into the depths of our heart and mind; it is also overwhelmingly powerful, summoning us to heroic acts and new ways of life. Important moments of our personal, individual life, as for the entire Church, can happen with startling abruptness. Peter finds himself, baptizing gentiles, not in order that they may receive the Holy Spirit but because they have already been graced by the Spirit in wonderful ways. Even though Peter was an observant Jew, like Jesus, obeying the dietary laws and other observances of his people, nonetheless, Peter could not refuse baptism for a single moment. Without instructing the gentiles in the Jewish law, he baptized them!

At the same time, there is a bond of family and continuity. Peter was challenged by other members of the Church and he explained his reason. We witness the need to continue who we are as a community of faith. The early Church will expend much energy, discussing still further this conclusion that gentiles can be received into the

*Following Sundays of the "A" cycle, John 10:11–18 is read.

Church without first becoming Jews. Paul will devote much of his energy to this theological question.

This movement, in the Church where questions are thrashed out theologically with an eye to tradition and earlier practices, and beyond the Church where new and unexpected manifestations of the Holy Spirit will startle us, was anticipated by Jesus in the parable of the Good Shepherd. In this story Jesus knows each of his sheep by name. He calls each one by a sound which reaches into the depths of their memory, all the way back to their birth when each one was given a name and a vocation for life. Each change in life, whether for the group or for the individual, must be kept in continuity not only with each person's past life but even with his ancestry from whom life and name have been received. Each change in life, moreover, must answer a personal call and touch a chord of love.

Because the Good Shepherd calls us by our name and leads us back and forth from our ancestry into our future, Jesus also compares himself to the door of the sheepfold. The means by which we go back and forth turns out to be Jesus himself. Through Jesus we slip backward into our subconscious, into the depths of life, and become absorbed in the mystery of our existence. We hear our name spoken by Jesus; we experience the betrothal of love and a union of ecstasy. Through Jesus, we pass through a door into our very best self, our name as spoken by Jesus.

Through this same door, which is Jesus, we are called to go forth into the activity of daily life, to mingle with other people, to form family, neighborhood and workcrew, schools and clubs, activities and plans. To hear Jesus summon us by name, and to pass through the gate which is Himself, we go beyond the sheepfold into the wider world about us. Here we are led to quench our thirst. Yet, at sundown we pass again through the same door, which is Jesus, as the sound of our name is spoken by the same Good Shepherd, and we are led back into the depths of ourselves, in silent prayer, in sleep.

In all this movement, as in all this rest, Jesus is at the center, and yet Jesus loses himself in us. He calls *our* name in order to summon us forth to nourishment and pasture as well as to call us back to the silent prayer of the sheepfold. Jesus, in many ways so silent that we do not realize his presence, lays down his life for his sheep. He dies, in the same way that parents die within their children. Parents' hopes and dreams are so caught up within the lives of their children that the father and mother no longer seem to have their own existence. The Good Shepherd lays down his life for his sheep.

In all these extraordinary moments, when the spirit seems to act abruptly and to lead us beyond our expectations—as happened to Peter in Acts of the Apostles—when the spirit leads us to lay down our life as our best plans and ideals are lost within a family, a community or a church—these are the times when we hear our names best—*as spoken by Jesus.*

Prayer:

Lord, my soul is thirsting for you. When shall I go and behold your face? My thirst will be quenched, my hopes fulfilled, if only I hear you, my Good Shepherd, pronouncing my name. Then I will be at your holy place and you will be the God of my gladness and joy.

Tuesday—Fourth Week of Easter

Acts 11:19–26. Many gentiles are converted, especially through the preaching of those disciples who had been dispersed by the persecution that arose because of Stephen. Barnabas comes from Jerusalem, searches for Paul and brings him to Antioch. Here the disciples are first called Christians.

John 10:22–30. My sheep, says Jesus, hear my voice; no one snatches them out of my hand. Jesus adds: "the Father and I are one."

The initiative must come from God. Through Jesus God speaks our name and we follow Jesus. From him we receive eternal life, and through him we are caught up into the Holy Trinity. United with Jesus, we are united with Father and Spirit; as Jesus says: "The Father and I are one."

When Jesus speaks our names, he reaches into the depths of our person and proclaims who we are, in our hopes and ideals, in our talents and mystery of life. In the Bible "name" announces a divine vocation from God, that reaches into the future, in fact all the way into eternity. Jesus, therefore, puts energy into our hidden reserves of life, he gives direction to these talents, and he thus speaks our name in such a way that it draws us into eternity.

Little wonder, then, that no one can snatch one of these, Jesus' sheep, out of his hand. When such an intimate and all-inclusive relationship is established by God's initiative, we are caught! Yet, we are absorbed, not in something or someone alien to ourselves; we are not reduced to slavery. Rather, we are caught because Jesus speaks what is most genuine about ourselves and what is most attractive about our future.

Jesus speaks these profound words about the mystery of our life and the wonder of its eternal existence in answer to a question put to him by the crowd in the Temple. They had said rather abruptly to Jesus: "How long are you going to keep us in suspense? If you are really the Messiah, tell us so in plain words."

Yet, how can Jesus speak something as intimate as a person's name under such circumstances? These words from the crowd are bordering on the sarcastic. They are selfish. They intrude upon the privacy of Jesus. Questions like these prevent Jesus from drawing the people into the mystery of themselves as created and dreamed by God. The people are rejecting mystery; they want a plain answer. Yes or No! Are you the Messiah? If you are, then we can begin the revolt against Rome. . . .

God must take the initiative and speak a word that touches the mystery of our lives and our future. God can do this, only if we allow him the space to be gentle and gracious, probing and enticing, perceptive and contemplative.

These same qualities characterize the great apostle Barnabas. He is canonized a saint even during his lifetime by these words in Acts: "He encouraged them all . . . he himself was a good man filled with the Holy Spirit and with faith." Elsewhere, Luke had interpreted his name to mean "son of encouragement" (Acts 4:36). Originally named Joseph, he was called Barnabas most probably because of his eloquent and encouraging style of preaching the gospel.

This openness of Barnabas to God's gifts induced him to search for Paul and to bring him to Antioch. Humanly speaking, if it had not been for Barnabas, Paul may have been lost and buried in the silent sands of some contemplative desert! Taking a cue from the gospel, we can say that through Barnabas, Jesus called his sheep "Paul" by name and led him into a career that was to transform the missionary enterprise of the Church and thereby the very nature of the Church.

This spread of the Church, we notice in Acts, came about, first as a reaction to the violent persecution of the Church at Jerusalem. This danger to life caused many of the disciples to flee to gentile territory. Through them a great impact was made upon the Jewish community at Antioch where many joined the disciples and became known, for the first time, as "Christians." The reaction, then, from violence to peace, and the reenforcement of this peace through the gentle encouragement of Barnabas, enabled Jesus to name his sheep and to draw them into discipleship.

We need to ask ourselves: do we manifest the gentleness which allows others to hear, through us, the pronunciation of their name by Jesus? Are we an instrument by which people, our family and neighbors, our friends at work or in other associations, begin to perceive the wonder of themselves as dreamed by God? Can they begin to look into their future with a sense of joy of the wonder that lies ahead?

Prayer:

Lord, speak my name, the mystery of your Father's creation in me. Through me, speak the secret name of my family and community. Allow me to be your gentle disciple, so that by my encouragement others are drawn into the wonder of hopes and possibilities which you have placed in them. Then all nations will praise you, O Lord, and will find their home in your holy city, the heavenly Jerusalem. As we praise you now, the goodness of that city will surround us now in our earthly life.

Wednesday—Fourth Week of Easter

Acts 12:24–13:5. After prayer and fasting, Barnabas and
Paul are commissioned by the church at Antioch to
undertake the first missionary journey. They arrive by
boat at Cyprus and begin preaching in the Jewish synagogues.

John 12:44–50. Jesus' words and work are commissioned
by the Father who sent him and so they are the source
of eternal life.

We glimpse the intimate community of life, between
Jesus and his heavenly Father, between the members of
the church at Antioch among themselves and with God.
Even though Jesus is the eternal Son of the heavenly Father, equal to the Father in all things, sharing the Father's wisdom and power, still Jesus does nothing on his
own.

> For I have not spoken on my own;
> no, the Father who sent me
> has commanded me
> what to say and how to speak.

Somehow or other, Jesus' entire existence, even his per-
sonality is formed by this obedient regard to the Father,
this receptivity to the Father's will and wisdom, this total
community of life with the Father.

In the church at Antioch, the community gathers
for liturgy while fasting from food and drink. Fasting
would leave the deep impression that their strength
comes from God, not from themselves nor from earthly
substance. Fasting also induces a bond of compassion, a
willingness to suffer together, a sense of being one with

all the world's poor and oppressed. As such, they are thoroughly open to God for guidance and for strength.

At this time of the liturgy, the Holy Spirit inspires a prophecy: "Set apart Barnabas and Saul." The language reminds us of the great prophets, like Jeremiah, called and set apart from his mother's womb, or the Suffering Servant of Isaiah, called from birth to be a light to the nations (Jer 1:5; Is 49:6).

Through Barnabas and Paul a new and wider community is to be established. The bond of Jesus' disciples is to spread across the Roman empire, during this first missionary journey to the island of Cyprus. The Holy Spirit did not give precise, detailed instructions—only a call to proceed forward on the journey. At first they proclaim the word of God in the Jewish synagogues. Yet, all the while God's main purpose was to attract more and more gentiles so that Christianity can bring the message of Moses, the prophets and Jesus to all the world.

Just as Jesus and the Father formed one intimate life, just as the disciples at Antioch were united among themselves and with the Holy Spirit, likewise the church at Antioch was to reach outward toward the world as one family in Christ.

At the heart of this growing circle and ever increasing family there abides the word of life from the heavenly Father. It is this outreach toward others in love that keeps us from over-controlling the word of God. As we share this word with others, it always seems to become something new, fresh, demanding, upsetting—the result whenever new life is added to any family. Yet, this life is but a continuity of life within the parents, which reaches back to the word which the Father speaks and Jesus hears.

If we remain too close-knit, then we can control and

thoroughly understand—or we think that we do. The outreach to the gentile world brought a whole new dimension to the ancient Bible. Almost every sentence had to be rethought within a new context. And when the church at Antioch, as earlier when the church at Jerusalem thought to have everything in good enough order, it was someone who reached outwards toward the nations that broke the order and yet enabled the profound mystery of God to remain just that, a mystery.

This mystery of God's hidden message, spoken wondrously in Jesus and heard through the prophets within our midst, is the most demanding voice that we will ever hear. It comes from the Father, communicated through Jesus, and continuously kept alive in the Church by the Holy Spirit; it reaches into the depth of ourselves as we have been created and endowed with life and with a future beyond our hopes. If our plans and human devices put such firm hands upon this mystery, that the wonder is lost and everything is humanly understandable, then we have lost our way and muffled the voice of the Holy Spirit. This human control is usually broken most forcefully by charity that reaches outward and sends us on a missionary journey of kindness to others.

Prayer:

Jesus, let all the world exult. Let the strangers who pass me by in silence be happy. Let all these mysterious parts of life become your instruments to bring me in touch again with the mystery that is you and your holy presence in my life. Then I too will exult and be glad with the nations.

Thursday—Fourth Week of Easter

Acts 13:13–25. Jesus fulfills the promise invested in the Davidic dynasty. John the Baptist pointed him out and anointed him.

John 13:16–21. No messengers outrank the one who sends them forth. Whoever receives a messenger, receives the one who sends him forth.

Putting the two readings together, a line of continuity stretches from eternity to earth and through Israel's history upon planet earth. Jesus is sent by the heavenly Father, with a message not just in words but in his very person. Jesus *is* that message drawn from the heart and intense life of the Godhead; Jesus, therefore, is the great I AM. This title, I AM, not only identifies Jesus with the eternal Godhead, but it also involves Jesus in the long history of Israel. God had revealed himself to Moses at the burning bush as the mysterious I AM (Ex 3:14).

"I am who I am, always there with you"—such is the sacred name for God in an extended, descriptive form. Put into the third person, it reads: "He who is always with you." As such, it was received in the Hebrew form of Yahweh.

Thus God revealed himself to Moses: the one who will always be with his people. In some way God's presence and merciful, strong interaction with the lives of his people determine who is God: *He is* what they are in their questions and answers, their hopes and struggles and triumphs. This sacred name is accepted by Jesus as his own: "that . . . you may believe that I AM."

Jesus then was absorbing into himself the entire history of Israel, and when Jesus was born of the virgin Mary, this entire history became incarnate, flesh and blood, in Jesus.

While preaching in the synagogue at Pisidian Antioch (different city from the Antioch in Acts 11:19), Paul reviews many of the great moments of Israel's history, with special attention to Moses, David and John the Baptist. The line of continuity then extended firmly from the Godhead, to earth, from the Patriarchs and Moses to David, from David to John the Baptist, from John the Baptist to "the one who comes after me [whose sandal] I am not worthy to unfasten."

Within this very observable line, from God to Jesus all through Israel's long history, some very evident disruptions leap forward, and new settlements occur. Israel is persecuted and oppressed with hard labor in Egypt. The land of promise was delayed for the forty years while they wandered almost aimlessly in the desert and then it had to be acquired by conquest and by a long period of taking root. Saul was rejected as king; and when Jesus appeared, the Davidic dynasty had disappeared from history. This series of up's and down's, of rejection and rehabilitation, continues front stage with Jesus. One of his own disciples betrayed him. Jesus stated: "He who partook of bread with me has raised his heel against me."

Immediately after announcing his betrayal, Jesus added:

I tell you this now before it takes place, so that when it takes place you may know that I AM.

Disruption, even violent change of plans, cut across the line of continuity from God to earth and from the early moments of Israel's history till Jesus appeared, and even within the life of Jesus such explosions marked the very presence of God: "that ... you may believe that I AM."

At first, such interruptions would seem to be the

work of the devil. Certainly Jesus' betrayal by Judas Iscariot is attributed to his possession by Satan (Luke 22:3). Yet, if we remember that God's plans are mysterious and beyond our total comprehension, that at crucial moments God takes over and brings us to decisions, attitudes and insights, to heights of wisdom and depths of strength, then it is not difficult to realize how we will suddenly move in ways never anticipated ahead of time. Or circumstances will converge in ways that leave us breathless. Maybe like Jesus, we feel betrayed by forces beyond our control.

At such moments God's providence is reaching its fulfillment. There can be no doubt that God is in control. We ourselves have lost control! It is not that we are totally passive. Like Paul at Pisidian Antioch, we need to turn to the Scriptures. And with the example of Paul we turn to the congregation at prayer. Jesus shows us how to turn one's thoughts to God and to share these perceptions with others. And as we live in this community or family setting, the lines of continuity return. We realize that God has sent his servants into our lives; that God has directed all the events. We believe and are at peace.

Prayer:

Lord, for ever I will sing your goodness. No matter what happens, when or how, I believe that your faithfulness is manifest. You are always my rock of strength, my Savior, the arm that makes me strong and secure.

Friday—Fourth Week of Easter

Acts 13:26–33. Paul's sermon in the synagogue at Pisidian Antioch continues. He states the fulfillment of the
Hebrew Scriptures in Jesus' death and resurrection, a
fulfillment which included human plans that seemed to
cut across God's will for goodness and justice among
his human family.

John 14:1–6. Jesus is going to prepare a place for us; he is
the way toward that place as well as the truth and the
life of us pilgrims.

So long as we live on planet earth, we have not arrived. "Here we have no lasting city" (Heb 13:14). While
Scripture accepts the fact that earth and even our entire
solar system can wear out and disintegrate, still it emphasizes far more the ephemeral, short-lived, ever changing
circumstances of our individual lives and of our society.
We are always on the way, seeking and looking beyond
where we are, following a hope. No sooner do we master
the situation of being a child than we are growing into
youth; just as soon as we grow out of the awkwardness of
youth, we have passed the border into adulthood. "Here
we have no lasting city." We are always on the way.

This situation can be exciting for younger people
with few responsibilities and with good physical health
and emotional expansiveness, to move from one thing to
another, from one person to another. Yet, for an older
person, with commitments in marriage, religious life,
priesthood and other careers, with a more settled disposi-
tion and less elastic spontaneity in new directions, it is
more and more frightening to be always on the way, always leaving something and someone behind for someone
or something new.

Here we are consoled by the words of Jesus: "I am

the way, and the truth, and the life." Somehow or other, to be seeking is to be found, to be on the way is to have arrived. To be straining one's eyes and hopes for Jesus means that we have already been found by Jesus. He is attracting us before we feel inclined to look for him. The flower must be found by sunlight before it will turn toward the sun.

To be on the way means to be seeking Jesus. We are longing to follow his will for peace, forgiveness, justice and compassion ever more totally in our daily life. To be on the way toward more profound peace or toward more extensive forgiveness or toward justice that shares earth's goodness with more and more of God's family, a journey such as this brings more security and delight. Most of all, in each step forward we find Jesus closer to ourselves in his personal love and attraction.

Still other paths stretch out before us, leading us on "the way." One of the most important of these exists in the Holy Scriptures. In today's epistle Paul concludes his journey through the Hebrew Bible, beginning with the patriarchs and Moses and ending with John the Baptist, the herald of Jesus. The earlier part of this journey was traversed in yesterday's reading. Today, in the latter part of the same speech at Pisidian Antioch, Paul hones in upon the congregation immediately before him.

First, we note how Paul swivels from the words of Scripture, inscribed upon a book or scroll, to those same words as spoken by the living God. All of Scripture, according to Paul, is to be read in the light of Jesus who gives the ultimate meaning to each statement. To go from words to a person, is to move from a clear statement to an unclear but forceful personal witness to those words. The process leads us from the intellect to the will, from mental work which divides and subdivides till it knows and controls, to a volitional and emotional response which is always much more difficult to grasp and still harder to control. Scripture then ought to become a springboard for contemplation, when in silent ecstasy we become lost in the wonder of Jesus' love and in an understanding beyond clear ideas.

Paul wrote about this "experience [of Christ's] ... love which surpasses all knowledge" (Eph 3:19).

We are on "the way," then, as we move from the words of Scripture to God or Jesus who speaks those words. We are also on "the way," strangely enough, when human sin or ignorance forces us out of our well-ordered plans into a vast and fearful waste (the words used in Deuteronomy for the way of the exodus from Egypt to the Promised Land!—Deut 1:19; 2:7). At such times, we are not to respond with hate nor with frustration. And when we feel helpless victims of evil, we can again be on "the way" with Jesus. By such a strange turn of circumstances, God hopes to share Israel's covenant with all the world. We too may be led thereby to share our best with many others, for the enrichment of all. That best is Jesus.

Prayer:

Each new turn along the way, Lord, leads toward a new birth. At all such moments I hear your words: "You are my child; this day I am begetting you." At such moments of new birth, give me the strength to be as obedient as any child in the moment of its birth.

Saturday—Fourth Week of Easter

Acts 13:44–52. Paul and Barnabas are rejected by the synagogue, or at least by influential people in it, and so they pass on to evangelize the gentiles.

John 14:7–14. Whoever believes that Jesus has come forth from the Father will not only accomplish the works of Jesus, but (Jesus adds) works "greater far than these."

We find a movement of God's presence, first in the solemn majesty and mysterious wonder of heaven, also in the manifestation of the Godhead on earth in the person of Jesus, then from God's word and presence among the Jewish people to an opening across the world. Once the grandeur of God's gift is realized, at that moment it must be shared with others. In allowing others, even strangers and foreigners, to sit down with us at the banquet table of God's presence, our family is transformed into something new and different. Just as the eternal word of God, incarnate in the womb of Mary, takes on an entirely new way of life—Jewish, Palestinian, Aramaic language, black hair, dark complexion, more emotional and less philosophical than the Greeks, more prophetical and less legal than the Romans—a similar evolution took place when the gospel migrated from an entirely Jewish setting to that of the Greek-Roman world.

Changes such as this can be extremely difficult, threatening and even divisive—as the Roman Catholic Church is experiencing in the wake of Vatican II—yet such a movement can also be a way of fulfilling Jesus' words to the apostle Philip: "The one who believes in me will do the works I do, and *greater far than these.*" How can *our* human works be greater than those of Jesus? Is Jesus teasing us with a bit of unreal praise or is he providing us with the scintillating opportunity of living in a never-never land for a few blissful moments?

These words in John's gospel may be reaching into the deep subconscious of Jesus and expressing something that parents often think and say to their children: what I couldn't do, you must do! You take my dreams and make them real. Jesus must have dreamed of a mission to the entire world and yet for many reasons was inhibited from acting upon it. He told the Canaanite woman, as he was journeying in "the district of Tyre and Sidon" outside the living area of the Jewish people: "My mission is only to the lost sheep of the house of Israel." And when she persisted, Jesus even stood his ground against her argument. Finally Jesus admitted: "Woman, you have great faith! Your wish will come to pass" (Matt 15:21–28). Your wish, Jesus seemed to say, is my wish—how I long to see us all one, joined around the heavenly banquet table. No one would then survive simply from the crumbs that fall to the ground!

As Jesus reached outward, often more instinctively than with clear precision of what was happening, he came into trouble with those who gave a very strict interpretation to the Mosaic laws and traditions. The transition from one family to another, from one world to another, was almost as dramatic as the moment of Jesus' incarnation, when the eternal word began to exist as Jesus, son of Mary, the Jewish maiden of Nazareth. Perhaps the Church's mission was still more dramatic, a work greater by far than anything which he had accomplished. Such changes are traumatic for many people, and eventually it cost Jesus his life, for it brought him into trouble with the religious leaders of his own people and with the civil authorities of Rome.

At Pisidian Antioch, where Paul has been living and

preaching, the great instinctive dream of Jesus came true—and again with a violent thrust of the sword that divided families and friends, that involved religious and civil authorities (Luke 12:51–53). Paul and Barnabas were excommunicated from the synagogue and expelled from the territory. On this occasion Paul quoted from the prophet Isaiah: "I have made you a light to the nations, a means of salvation to the ends of the world."

Our life too changes, at times with traumatic drama, at other times with agony, and still again with scintillating joy. These transitional moments usually come unexpectedly with demands that seem exorbitant and even unreasonable. They change our life, upsetting our security. Not only are we asked to share our finest joys and most precious hopes with others, but others will make something different of them than we intended. Just as when Judaism became Christianity and the eternal God became human, our whole self is transformed by what others do with our gift.

Such moments occur: as we grow from youth to adult life, from single life to marriage, religious vocation and priesthood, from health to sickness, from independence to helpless old age, from earthly to heavenly existence. These are the way to the Father, the works greater than those of Jesus' own lifetime, the light and consolation of others. We can reread today's Scripture in the context of any personal crisis.

Prayer:

Jesus, you share your vocation with each of us. As you were the light to the nations, we too are asked to open our hands and our hearts and to offer to others the best that we have and are. As we become a light to others, enable us not only to be calm, but even joyful as other people color and transform that light, just as earth transformed the light that you were from all eternity in heaven.

Monday—Fifth Week of Easter

Acts 14:5–18. After forced to leave Iconium by an intrigue against their lives, Paul and Barnabas came to Lystra where they cured a crippled man who listened to Paul's preaching and had faith to be saved. Paul and Barnabas then had to resist the people who wanted to sacrifice to them as though they were gods.

John 14:21–26. If anyone obeys the commandments of the Lord, that person will be loved by the Father and by Jesus. "We will come to that one and make our dwelling there." "The Holy Spirit . . . will instruct you in everything."

As we energetically begin a day or a project, we really want to be instructed by the Holy Spirit *"in everything."* Then, we will be such instruments of the Spirit, that people will sense the power of miracles within us, as once they did within Paul. And as we look at others, even if they are crippled in body or in mind, we too like Paul will see a faith strong enough to heal them of their infirmity. Today's Scriptures instruct us on ways to arrive at this change and expression of the Holy Spirit.

First, we must be obedient to the Holy Spirit. The least desire of God must become a commandment of love. To disobey is to be destroyed. Commandments then are not a set of difficult rules but an assurance that we are following God's holy will, moment by moment. This same Holy Spirit will also remind us of everything that Jesus has spoken, and in doing so, the Spirit will revive hidden resolutions for prayer or forgiveness, for patience or helpfulness. All these earlier graces from Jesus, which at one time meant so much to us, will stir with fresh life. Somehow or other, we are brought back to the first moment of youth when life lay before us and we bounded with all sorts of wonderful ideas. The Holy Spirit, then, touches us where we are at our best, God's masterpiece, a creation of love, meant to be an instrument of love toward others, and so to reveal the wonderful presence of God.

Jesus' word, which the Holy Spirit enables us to hear as though spoken for the first time, brings us into the cycle of God's magnificent life. This word comes from the Father and therefore as Jesus confessed, "is not mine." It sends Jesus forth on his ministry of world salvation, drawing him into desert nights of prayer, inspiring him to teach and to heal. It reaches us today in the Scriptures and through the Scriptures articulates the words of the Spirit within our spirit. It animates our hidden hopes and good ambitions. Thus the word sustains a cycle of divine life, from heaven to earth and back again to heaven. That word then has left its traces in our created universe and in our memories and subconscious. St. Paul expressed it this way in today's reading:

> We are bringing you the good news that will convert you . . . to the living God, "the one who made heaven and earth and the sea and all that is in them." . . . In bestowing his benefits, he has not hidden himself without a clue. From the heavens he sends down rain and rich harvests; your spirits he fills with food and delight.

The *second* condition or suggestion from today's Scripture reading, enabling us to be instruments of the

Spirit within our community and family, rests upon the strong faith that God's word is written *everywhere*. The Word (with capital W) within the Scriptures makes the other words intelligent and forceful.

A *third* condition is imbedded within the second. If the word is everywhere, then it belongs to everyone. It can never be heard and then captured as an individual's private property. By its nature it must be shared or it dies. Just as the Father's word, according to Jesus, "is not mine. It comes from the Father who sent me . . . [to] instruct you in everything," likewise the word which we perceive in our hearts and in our world must continuously flow through us to inspire new life in others.

Fourthly, this life-giving, life-restoring word must be received, not only obediently (as we mentioned earlier) but also unconditionally. We must not put boundaries or conditions upon it—otherwise (again) it dies! To put this aspect of the word as clearly as possible, we must be convinced that we can be God's instrument—through the word—in working miracles. As we speak the Word (with a capital W) that absorbs and transforms all of our words (with a small w)—that is, as God's inspired Word infuses new life into all our thoughts and expressions, others must respond like the crippled man at Lystra. They look on us and see in us "the faith to be saved." How can such a moment happen? Jesus answers:

The Paraclete, the Holy Spirit,
whom the Father will send in my name,
will instruct you in everything.

Prayer:

Lord Jesus, increase our faith. Grant us an obedient spirit, enlivened by the Holy Spirit, so that we can read your word inscribed across the universe and deeply within our hearts. Then we can share that Word with all your family on earth. All of us will be miracle workers to each other.

Tuesday—Fifth Week of Easter

Acts 14:19–28. Paul is stoned at Lystra but saved by the intervention of his disciples. As he completes with Barnabas the first great missionary journey, Paul speaks of the necessity of undergoing many trials and of the door being opened toward the gentiles.

John 14:27–31. Jesus' farewell gift of peace. We ought to rejoice that Jesus returns to the Father. Thus the world will know that Jesus loves the Father and does as the Father has commanded.

Jesus speaks of going away. He will return to the Father. He has come forth in obedience to the Father's will, and now at the bidding of God the Father Jesus directs his face toward the cross, resurrection and ascension. He will be reunited with the Father and the Spirit.

Earlier, during last Saturday's gospel for the Fourth Week of Easter, Philip had questioned Jesus. "Show us the Father," Philip remonstrated, "and that will be enough for us." Still earlier in the preceding day's gospel, Thomas argued with Jesus: "Lord, we do not know where you are going. How can we know the way?" In one sense, the disciples cannot follow Jesus. And in still another sense, they must walk in the footsteps of Jesus. Jesus had said, again during the gospel of last Friday, "I am going to prepare a place for you . . . I am the way."

One of the ways by which we follow Jesus, into his mysterious life with the Father and the Spirit, is to allow our own spirit come to rest in the deepest part of ourselves. Here is where the temple of God is constructed; here is the Holy of Holies of that temple, here resides the Ark of the Covenant, containing the tablets of the law (Deut 31:26). Here is where we hear God's word, the "commandment" that requires immediate obedience, as was discussed yesterday. For if God really and truly speaks, we have no choice, only one of life or death. To disobey would be to destroy our very selves as created by God.

Before this Holy of Holies, the seraphim continually call out: "Holy, holy, holy is the Lord of hosts—*Qadosh! Qadosh! Qadosh yahweh seba'oth!*" Holy—in the Hebrew *qadosh*—means separation, overwhelming distance, awesome transcendence, as fearful as approaching the sun, as murky and black as the bottom of the ocean. Yet, this same God speaks with us and calls us "friend!" We can approach this God—we can fly into the sun and sink to ocean depths. The more personal is God's embrace, the more profound is our ecstasy of love. Jesus is the way to the Father. We can know that way only by faith, and faith means a surrender out of love to the unknown. This unknown aspect of faith becomes all the more mysterious and undecipherable because it is not a quality of an object but the love of a person. That person is God, Father, Son and Spirit.

When we settle into the depths of ourselves, we hear God speak our name, like the Creator calling us into existence. This word, ourselves, is spoken in the same dark, mysterious, wondrous, thoroughly personal and still overwhelmingly transcendent way that a child is conceived. God speaks our name and we are created. We must let our spirit come to rest at the depths of ourselves, so that we can hear that name, that word of ourselves, spoken again, with the pure strong accents of God's voice.

At such moments we experience a peace beyond words, a peace that the world cannot give, as Jesus says in today's gospel.

Within such eternal moments of peace, God calls us forth into new life. Like Paul and Barnabas the door is opened for us to move through "foreign" lands and to live with "gentiles." Through the word of God, we absorb new strength and new wisdom. Our most hidden hopes come alive. Our ideals, that once frightened us because of their weird unreality, take on the force of a divine commandment; they are spoken anew by God.

Surrendering to such ideals means suffering! As St. Paul said to the Christian community of Antioch [where Peter was in charge for a while]:

We must undergo many trials if we are to enter into the reign of God.

Paul could speak from experience. He had just been stoned and left for dead at Pisidian Antioch [farther north than the other Antioch]. Yet, it may be possible that Paul suffered less from the stoning than he did from the demand of God to forgive those who stoned him. It must have been far easier for Paul to put up with persecution than to bear with jealousy which prompted the persecution.

We are called by Jesus to peace. And peace means forgiving others, bearing with other's differences, even their misunderstanding and jealousy.

Peace is my farewell to you,
my peace is my gift to you;
I do not give it to you as the world gives
         peace.
Do not be distressed or fearful.

Prayer:

Jesus, you ask us not to be fearful in the midst of fear, not to be distressed when we are opposed, even persecuted. We can know what you mean only by following your way. Give us the strength, so that we surrender our spirits to you and go along your way to the Father where we hear the divine revelation, which is ourselves, our names.

Wednesday—Fifth Week of Easter

Acts 15:1–6. Because some Jewish Christians demanded circumcision of gentile converts, Paul and Barnabas went up to Jerusalem where the apostles and elders decided to call an assembly to decide the question.

John 15:1–8. Jesus said: I am the vine, you are the branches ... Without me you can do nothing. If you live in me, whatever you ask the Father in my name will be done for you.

Each biblical reading reaches into the roots and sources of life and calls upon us to locate our origins in Jesus. For the Jewish people circumcision was the seal of the covenant, not only upon the flesh but also upon the transmission of life. Through this mark, the Jewish people not only reached back to their ancestor, the patriarch Abraham (Gen 15), but they also manifested their willingness to be known as a follower of Moses, and if need be, to die out of loyalty to the covenant of Mount Sinai. Circumcision then was much more than a ceremony. It was a family and ancestral symbol of loyalty to one another and to Yahweh, the God of their ancestors, who united them as his very own people (Ex 19:5–6).

Jesus, we learn in the gospel of Luke, was circumcised on the eighth day after his birth (Luke 2:21). So was St. Paul (Phil 3:5). Each, therefore, followed the Mosaic law scrupulously. Jesus may have differed with some of the Jewish groups like the Pharisees about the interpretation of the law and about the binding force of some traditions. Yet, Jesus himself told his followers to obey the rules set down by the priests, even if the priests' example was not worthy of imitation (Matt 23:3).

Circumcision then reached into the roots and sources of life where bonds of love and loyalty were maintained between the people and with their God. And Jesus belonged at the heart of this relationship.

Jesus, moreover, said: I am the vine, you are the branches. We have already learned from the gospel that Jesus is the Way whose footsteps we are to follow. The question became very serious: was circumcision to be required of all Christian converts, if they were male? And if female, were they required to undergo the ceremonial bath and to follow the strict dietary laws?

This question has long been settled within Christianity. Paul's theology triumphed, claiming that Jesus had brought the Old Law to its finality and fulfillment. Because of Jesus' birth, death and resurrection, it was no longer necessary first to be a Jew in order to become a Christian. Yet, the revolutionary effect of this question upon early Christianity and its relation with Judaism has a continuing impact upon our lives and decisions today.

When the scriptures force us to think deeply—to return to the roots and sources of life—we are brought into contact with the basic issues of life and death. As a result, all other questions fall away. We can no longer nitpick at small things, argue about pennies and nickels, force an ultimatum for reasons of personal pride. Heroic decisions are asked, yea demanded of us. These decisions may be as crucial as healing family feuds, going the extra mile to retrieve a friend, taking great risks and even financial losses to bring a true Christian environment into one's family, answering the call to prayer, day by day, at ever longer periods of time, awakening a new awareness to the many social injustices in our society. These kinds of decisions reach so deeply that they are bound to transform our attitudes and our external life style. They will influence our circle of friends, separating us from some and making new friends of others.

These are the moments when we realize how desperately we rely upon Jesus. As we act courageously upon these inspirations, we realize ever more forcefully that the spirit is not our own; it is the spirit of Jesus. Now we know that Jesus is the vine, we are the branches. Deep in our heart, we know for certain that Jesus has been inspiring these desires and hopes, that Jesus has been strengthening us in our long travail of decision-making, that Jesus has brought these secret hopes to extraordinary fulfillment. Jesus says: without me you can do nothing. We can now add: with Jesus we can do everything.

When we are thus servants of the spirit—a spirit that is at once Jesus' and our own, a spirit that is like the sap which flows from vine to branches and back again—then Jesus says also to us:

> If you live in me
> and my words stay part of you,

you may ask what you will—
it will be done for you.
My Father has been glorified
in your bearing much fruit
and becoming my disciples.

In this wondrous interchange of life, we are challenged by the Spirit of Jesus to follow through with mo-
mentous decisions. Just as the early Church could reach
beyond the practice of Jesus and no longer demand circumcision, we too are being asked to leap forward from
ideas and devotions that separated us from others and to
make heroic decisions of forgiveness, patience, social justice and concern for the oppressed, a thoroughly Christian homelife. Then, our own hopes can be trusted as divinely inspired and we can be confident: you may ask
what you will—it will be done for you. When we live this
deeply—at the roots—in God, then there is an immedi-
acy and certainty of God's force and direction in life.

Prayer:
Lord Jesus, prune away the vine. Cut off the dry
branches. Remove everything that separates us from you
and from our brothers and sisters in the family of the human race. Let us all together be united firmly with you
and with one another, as vine and branch, in one flow of
spirit and life. Then we can know the glory of trusting
our deepest hopes as truly from you.

Thursday—Fifth Week of Easter

Acts 15:7–21. At the Jerusalem council a decision was reached not to place any further burdens on the gentiles except some "customary" practices important to the Jewish Christians. The gentiles' hearts have been purified by faith and the gift of the Spirit. They are being saved by the favor of Jesus Christ.

John 15:9–11. As the Father has loved me, Jesus says, so have I loved you. Live on in my love, keep my commandments and your joy will be complete.

A spontaneous interchange of life, love and joy flows between God the Father and God the Son. This force which attracts and unites them is so personal and real as to be God the Holy Spirit. Jesus desires that this same bond exist between ourselves and his own person.

> As the Father has loved me,
> so have I loved you.
> Live on in my love.
> My joy may be yours
> and your joy may be complete.

This spirit of love and enthusiasm was found to exist among non-baptized gentiles by Peter and Paul. What Jesus had prayed to come among his disciples, was already present among foreigners even before their baptism. Peter was referring to the "second Pentecost" when the Holy Spirit descended upon the household of Cornelius, a non-baptized Roman, in almost the same way as when the Spirit came upon the first disciples of Jesus in the supper room (Acts 1:13, 2:1). We read in Acts:

> Peter had not finished these words when the
> Holy Spirit descended upon all who were listen-

ing to Peter's message. The circumcised believers who had accompanied Peter were surprised that the gift of the Holy Spirit should have been poured out on the gentiles also, whom they could hear speaking in tongues and glorifying God (Acts 10:44–46).

Peter, therefore, directed that these people be baptized at once in the name of Jesus Christ. These pagan Romans were not required first to be circumcised, to undergo ceremonial baths and to obey dietary laws among the Jewish people. To baptize the pagans immediately seemed like a command from Jesus, even though Jesus himself had submitted to circumcision and other Mosaic prescriptions.

We all experience moments, like those which suddenly came upon Peter and Paul in the apostolate, when we are faced with a *fait accompli*, the accomplished fact of a person manifesting undeniable gifts of the Spirit and yet thinking and acting in a way different from our own tradition and customs, maybe even opposed to our ways. These people are sincere, authentic, gifted with common sense, yet unable to agree with us. These "gentiles" receive the spirit in a way that clashes with our own traditions and customs. To put it as bluntly as possible, God's way of acting in them seems (to our way of judging) to break God's laws! Perhaps, we think to ourselves: these people are mistaken and therefore cannot be directed by the spirit of Jesus. Or, they are partially right and partially wrong, partially good and sincere and partially blinded and biased. Yet, every human being combines these strange opposites. At the same time it is not possible at the moment to pull the threads apart and separate the good from the bad, the correct from the erroneous, as we interact with these "gentiles."

The Scriptures offer us some good advice. First, let us never deny the existence of the Holy Spirit whenever we see a manifestation of affection, concern, patience, and self-sacrifice for the sake of others. These are undeniable gifts of the spirit, no matter what faults, errors and misconceptions also lodge in the same person. Certainly the gentiles of the household of Cornelius, baptized immediately by Peter, still clung to many pagan, superstitious ideas. There is good reason to think that their moral principles did not measure up to those of the first disciples of Jesus. Yet, Peter ordered baptism immediately. And later Paul defended this action as a policy for the Church.

Yet, in the decision reached at Jerusalem, a second piece of advice was given. The gentiles were required to respect some deeply imbedded sensitivities of the Jewish people. These were customary procedures all related to blood: not to undertake marriage with certain close relatives; not to partake of blood whether directly, or indirectly in animals improperly butchered; and not to purchase meat from the common market as it had not only been offered to pagan gods but had not been correctly drained of blood. Therefore, expectations were rightly made on both sides, even today, by which people show a gentle, calm consideration for the customs and impressions of others. Conversion, therefore, is not simply a theological debate; it is a reconciliation with a family where Jesus is the head.

Finally, in his response at the Jerusalem council, James quoted from the prophet Amos to find a foreshadowing of this future conversion of the gentiles. James, however, did not quote verbatim from the Hebrew Scriptures. After repeating that God "will raise up the fallen house of David" he omitted the next line, "that they may conquer what is left of [the gentile people of] Edom." James omitted the military conquest, forcing gentiles to submit to God's chosen people. James, therefore, adapted the Hebrew Scriptures to a development which took place with Jesus who avoided political and especially military confrontations. Jesus separated himself from the political implications of the kingdom of David and spoke rather of the kingdom of God. James reached into Scripture to understand better the surprising gift of the spirit to gentiles. Yet, his Scripture was the *living* and therefore the evolving word of God. We too when faced with serious differences, yet also with the evident manifestation of the good spirit of Jesus in others, ought to reach into tradition and into the Scriptures for guidance.

Conversion in the Spirit, therefore, is much more than a theological victory; it is reconciliation within a family, the household of the faith. Then as Jesus says in the gospel: "My joy may be yours and your joy may be complete."

Prayer:

Lord Jesus, grant us a good eye, always to see what is good in others, despite the differences between us. Help us so to read the Scriptures, that we can appreciate your Holy Spirit in others, even when there is an initial clash. Let all our actions prepare for a conversion that reunites your family in all its members.

Friday—Fifth Week of Easter

Acts 15:22–31. After the Council of Jerusalem, the gentiles are given directions, so as not to antagonize the Jewish Christians who followed the Mosaic law.

John 15:12–17. Love one another as I have loved you. You have not chosen me; I have chosen you.

Today's biblical readings combine human compromise along with heroic expectations. Heroically, we are to love one another as Jesus has loved us and has laid down his life for us. Such extensive and demanding loyalty was preached within the early Church, which also arrived at an heroic compromise: gentiles are not required to follow what seemed essential laws of Judaism (like circumcision and dietary rules) yet they were asked to maintain certain customary procedures, like not eating the meat of strangled animals (see yesterday's meditation). Both the compromise decision of the Jerusalem Council and the willingness to die for one's friends are attributed to the promptings of the Holy Spirit.

We will all agree that martyrdom must be inspired by the Spirit of God, but we often think of compromise as at least slightly immoral and almost always as a decline in personal ideals. Yet the letter of the Jerusalem Council begins: "It is the decision of the *Holy Spirit* and ours too, not to lay any burden beyond that which is *strictly* necessary. . . . " The word in italics, *strictly,* indicates some kind of minimalist interpretation.

The Jerusalem Council helped to solve one of the most serious threats ever encountered by the Church. If it had repudiated Paul's action (of not requiring circumcision and dispensing gentile converts from the full Jewish law), Christianity would have remained a small sect within the Roman Empire, a satellite of Judaism, and

never what Jesus intended as the fulfillment of all prophecies and hopes, the new covenant promised by Jeremiah
and Ezekiel (Jer 31:31–34; Ez 36:22–28), the final age of
the world. This decision had not been clearly made by Jesus himself. Although Jesus gave hints or signals of a
world religion, breaking the bonds of the practice of the
ancestral religion in his days, still his clear statement almost said the opposite: he instructed his twelve disciples:
"Do not visit pagan territory and do not enter a Samaritan town. Go instead after the lost sheep of the house of
Israel" (Matt 10:5–6). Jesus likewise defended himself before the requests of the Canaanite woman: "My mission
is only to the lost sheep of the house of Israel" (Matt
15:24). Paul's struggle to win acceptance in the Church
for his own "liberal" position (many in the early Church
called it heretical, and even Peter weakened—Gal 2:11–
14) is clear enough proof that Jesus had left the question
undecided, perhaps unasked!

The Church faced this crucial test of her nature and
mission by calling an assembly of "the whole Jerusalem
church" with the apostles and elders. Their decision was
set by a letter placed in the hands of Paul and Barnabas
along with the leading men of the community, Judas,
known as Barsabbas, and Silas.

This letter bears all the marks of compromise and
diplomacy. First, the Jerusalem church states clearly that
it had not sent those "of our number" . . . [who] have upset you . . . and disturbed your peace of mind." Secondly,
the decision rests upon the principle, "not to lay on you
any burden beyond that which is strictly necessary." The
Council, therefore, followed the sunshine policy of open
discussion, so that everyone bore the responsibility of the
decision. It also voted for freedom wherever possible. It

asked for special consideration as regards certain Jewish customs where sensitivities were delicate.

Such a solution, at that moment, would fulfill the Lord's commandment: "Love one another as I have loved you ... [even to] laying down one's life for one's friends." The practice of patience can be heroic. To give in on unimportant details summons extraordinary humility. To discuss quietly an explosive issue and to remain at the conversation till a solution is reached manifest enormous trust in others' goodwill as in God's assistance.

Often enough very simple answers make all the difference between peace and war, whether among nations or among families and friends. How often, unfortunately, we are unwilling to listen and speak with calm perseverance, to give and to take, to barter and exchange, to be conscious of others' feelings and sensitivities, to forgive and forget quarrels and accusations.

The heroic compromise of the Jerusalem Council still must have been a serious blow at many Jewish Christians. Practices of piety and devotion, styles of worship and prayer, received from their ancestors and from Jesus himself, would no longer be binding upon the gentile Christians who very soon outnumbered the Jewish Christians. These same Christians of Hebrew origin would have been embarrassed before their Jewish relatives and friends who did not become followers or disciples of Jesus nor members of the Christian church. The torch was being passed to a new generation. It is a glorious moment; it is also a moment of heroic pain and separation. Jesus said to his disciples:

> This is my commandment: to lay down one's life for one's friends.

Prayer:

Jesus, I pray for patience, endurance, understanding. Give me a listening heart, a self-sacrificing spirit. Strengthen me to let loose of those small, precious, very personal, yet at times divisive aspects of my life. Make me an instrument of your peace.

Saturday—Fifth Week of Easter

Acts 16:1–10. In the midst of a new missionary journey, Paul is guided by the Spirit of Jesus, away from parts of Asia Minor and in the direction of Greece. Along the way Timothy joins Paul as a fellow missionary and for the sake of the Jewish people Paul has him circumcised.

John 15:18–21. The world will manifest hatred toward Jesus and toward his disciples. The people act this way, says Jesus, because "they know nothing of him who sent me."

Adversity continues to exert its important role in the apostolate. Persecuted in one place, the disciples fled to another place. And so the gospel moved onward and continued to spread across the Roman Empire. Whenever local conditions threw road blocks in Paul's way and kept him from preaching in the name of Jesus, the Scripture explains the situation thus: "They had been prevented *by the Holy Spirit* from preaching the message." This highly theological phrase, "prevented by the Holy Spirit," almost seems like a quieting and smothering blanket, spread over a snarling case involving intrigue, jealousy, fear, false ambition, such as we know to have happened in other places when the full documents are available, as for instance at Corinth (Acts 18; 1–2 Cor). While the apostolate proceeds within the full human setting, with its false judgment and selfish motivation, nonetheless, the Scriptures are always intent to recognize a *mystery* of salvation being achieved "by the Holy Spirit" through human instruments.

In the Scriptures the action of the Holy Spirit is almost always embracing human plans and prudent compromise. For instance, we read for today's selection from Acts that "Paul had him [namely Timothy] circumcised because of the Jews of that region." Yet, at the same time Paul was transmitting "to the people for observance the decisions which the apostles and elders had made in Jerusalem." Among these decisions was the clear stipulation that difficult burdens, like the rule of requiring circumcision before baptism, was not to be imposed, as we have already discussed in the preceding two meditations. Once Paul had settled the issue that circumcision was not necessary, then he felt free to circumcise! Paul's human plans, accordingly, included some rather sophisticated reasoning, some hard bargaining with the Jerusalem church, some staunch loyalty to principle, some provision for compromise on non-essentials. Now that circumcision was no longer an absolute prerequisite for salvation, Paul ignored this monumental victory and decided to have Timothy circumcised, if that young man was to be his assistant. Paul did this "because of the Jews of that region"!

Paul wanted to preserve a clear line of continuity with the Jewish ancestry of the Christian faith. He would act, even with diplomatic finesse and compromise; he would also act with stern dedication to principle. Through it all, Paul was conscious of being led by the Holy Spirit.

At other times this continuity would have to be

maintained in the midst of hostility and persecutions. Once again, this problem was handled variously. At times, hardships had to be faced directly, even to the point of martyrdom. Paul eventually died such a death, a heroic witness of his devotion and obedience to the Spirit. Paul could then have remembered the words of Jesus, as we hear them in today's gospel:

> If you find that the world hates you,
> know that it has hated me before you . . .
> You do not belong to the world.
> But I chose you out of the world. . . .
> They will harry you
> as they harried me.

To be chosen out of this world can reach the point of martyrdom.

At other times, to be chosen out of the world means to avoid Bithynia "the province of Asia" in preaching the gospel. We do not know the exact problems, but in any case Paul did not crash into them but went around them. And twice the decision—to be prudent and to compromise—is attributed to the Holy Spirit. In some way, Paul is being chosen "out of [or away from] the world"—of Asia and Bithynia—and in still another way Paul remained very much in the world, as the Spirit beckoned him to Macedonia.

"Beckoned to Macedonia" turns out to be a simple phrase, slipped almost unnoticed into the inspired text of the Bible. Yet, here is one of those monumental, most dramatic steps. Christianity passes into Europe. The heart of biblical religion will no longer be located at Jerusalem but somewhere else. The decision has not yet been made, of course, but the first step in its formulation has been taken. That step was induced by a set of human circumstances, some petty and insignificant yet all the while annoying, others much more theological and serious. Paul handled the situation with a combined reaction of stern principle and diplomatic compromise. All the while, he was convinced that he was being led by the Holy Spirit.

Prayer:

Jesus, grant us the wisdom to distinguish between a call to stand firm and a need to bend and compromise. And in the midst of difficulties which require one or other response, sharpen our eyes to realize your presence and open our ears to hear your voice. Give us the faith to realize that you are leading us and our Church in the fulfillment of your plans.

Monday—Sixth Week of Easter

Acts 16:11–15. Paul, Luke and perhaps others in Paul's company cross over to Greece, and at Philippi meet Lydia who is converted and asks Paul to remain in her household and to make it his headquarters.

John 15:25–16:4. As disciples of Jesus, we can endure persecution, even death for his name, because of the Spirit sent to us by Jesus.

Paul's life at Philippi at first settled down to one of exceptional peace. By contrast today's gospel anticipates persecutions and martyrdom, inflicted by those who do not know either the Father or the Son. Such is always the Church, at peace in some areas, rent apart by severe trials in other areas. If we experience happy tranquility, we must always remember those who are suffering and dying. If we are the victims of pain, separation and unreasonable—and seemingly useless—persecution, we should never lose heart; we also belong to a victorious, happy Church. Such contradictions are the normal conditions of life. Life, furthermore, can change quickly and dramatically, from serenity to anxiety and onward to baffling questions and deep agony. Paul, in fact, was experiencing such a striking transition in his life. Up till now in Asia Minor (more or less equivalent to modern Syria and Turkey), he had been plagued by Jewish Christians who challenged his credentials as an apostle and who contradicted his "gospel" (2 Cor 11–12) that faith in Jesus has set us free, particularly from the Mosaic prescriptions. Summoned by a vision to come to Macedonia (Greece), as we found in yesterday's reading, Paul stepped into a period of peace. In Greece, he moved rather quickly to the city of Philippi and was graciously received by a wealthy woman named Lydia, who offered the use of her home as his headquarters.

Paul literally fell in love with the Philippi church. His epistle to them is among the most touching in the Bible. He wrote:

> I give thanks to my God every time I think of you—which is constantly, in every prayer I utter—rejoicing, as I plead on your behalf, at the way you have all continually helped promote the gospel from the very first day ... I hold all of you dear ... God himself can testify how much I long for each of you with the affection of Christ Jesus! (Phil 1:3–8).

The passage from Acts, which describes in a bit more detail Paul's first days at Philippi, also helps to correct the misapprehension of Paul's misogyny. If he had been a fiercely outspoken anti-feminist, then a woman as sophisticated and discerning as Lydia—a wealthy merchant—should not have been won to Christianity by Paul's preaching and then here offered him the use of her own house.

Paul seemed to be surrounded with contentment and success, at least at first while living at Philippi. At the same time, in today's scriptural readings, John's gospel refers to the way that Christians were to be expelled from religious assemblies. They would be put to death by people who mistakenly claimed to be serving God. This clash in themes may seem unreal and unworkable, yet it is as real as life can be. Today, somewhere in the world, Christians are being expelled from their homes and from their churches, are being dragged before law courts and sentenced to long imprisonment and to death. Or their death may come less gloriously, as they rot away in confinement.

Perhaps in our own lives, part of ourselves must keep a joyful appearance, while another part of ourselves harbors a secret reservoir of pain, disappointment and doubt. All of us in one way or another, combine success and failure, achievement and frustration.

This combination has many advantages, and lest we forget, the liturgy puts the diverse situations clearly before us in today's two readings. God allows sorrow and disappointment to overshadow our lives so that our joy does not get out of hand and degenerate into forgetfulness of God, sensuality, indifference toward the needy and other forms of selfishness. Such sorrow enables us to be compassionate toward others in their suffering. Yet, this compassion is far more optimistic than a consoling drink of cool water before execution. It is compassion with hope and optimism. Life can be better, for in Jesus we have the reassuring words of someone who has suffered more than we endure.

In sorrow we intuitively feel the hope which comes to us from other parts of the Church, which is enjoying the peace and victory of Christ. As a result we can suffer more, be more compassionate, extend more hope, undertake new and greater trials for the sake of others. We can be convinced that we will never slip to any extreme and find ourselves cut off; the Church remembers all these experiences of life. In this embrace the Church encloses great suffering and overwhelming peace, not only the assurance that greater risks can be taken for the sake of others but also the realization that the Church will balance whatever may otherwise tend to extremes. The Spirit who prompts all good actions and who consoles all sorrowing people, that same Spirit comes to us from the Father and bears witness on behalf of Jesus.

Prayer:

Lord Jesus, we thank you for the Spirit of truth. This enables us to see a vision of the entire Church and of all the world. Our joys then can be shared with others who need our consolation; our sorrows are mitigated by the Church at peace. Your truth is that vast and it is the way to your wisdom and love.

Tuesday—Sixth Week of Easter

Acts 16:22–34. At Philippi Paul and Silas were arrested, flogged and imprisoned. When an earthquake shook the prison, its doors flew open. Paul and Silas did not flee. The jailer and his household were converted to faith in Jesus.

John 16:5–11. It is better, James says, that he return to the Father, so as to send the Paraclete. This Holy Spirit will convict the world of sin, justice, and condemnation.

Crises usually hit us by surprise. Seldom can we plan for them, particularly those which we have never before experienced. Suddenly, Paul's peaceful life at Philippi was shattered. We read earlier from the account in Acts, that Paul "became annoyed" with the girl who followed him, shouting, "These men are servants of the Most High God; they will make known to you a way of salvation." So, Paul "turned around and said to the spirit, 'In the name of Jesus Christ I command you, come out of her.' "

The account in Acts continues: "When her masters saw that their source of profit was gone" as this girl had brought substantial money to them by her fortune-telling, "they seized Paul and Silas and dragged them ... before the local authorities" and stirred up a mob who "joined in the attack."

We can sympathize with Paul's annoyance, but we can't help but wonder if a bit more patience and tolerance would have saved him a lot of trouble! Or perhaps Paul was stirred with pity for the unfortunate girl whom her masters used for their own profit. In any case, the whole situation changed dramatically for Paul and Silas.

In times of crises we discover hidden resources of strength and wisdom through our faith in Jesus. That Je-

sus should make the supreme difference is evident from
Acts. Paul was able to endure a punishment as torturous
as a public scourging. This punishment could not be inflicted upon a Roman citizen. In this case, Paul was later
to demand a public apology from the magistrates. Yet,
for the moment, Paul and Silas maintained an extraordinary calm. "About midnight ... Paul and Silas were
praying and singing hymns to God." Then another quick
change happened. An earthquake broke down the prison
gates. Paul and Silas could have fled away, yet they remained within the prison.

This calm strength was not possessed by the jailer.
He woke up, saw the prison gates wide open and drew his
sword to kill himself. He could not endure the disgrace of
losing his prisoners. Paul shouted: Do not harm yourself!
After a quick instruction about Jesus, Paul baptized the
jailer and his entire household. This man then spread a
feast to celebrate his newly found faith. It was not just
the decision of the prisoners not to run away that transformed a person in panic into a strong, steady man. The
Scriptures say that faith made the difference.

We too possess hidden resources of strength, if our
faith is strong and if we truly believe in Jesus' love and
power to save us. Then, like Paul, when a crisis hits unexpectedly, for instance a death in the family or community, our faith at once places us into the wide world of the
deceased in Purgatory or in Heaven. We do not flee from
the reality of our situation (we remain like Paul in prison), yet we can conquer death. In the Eucharist we recline with the saints and with the suffering souls in Purgatory, just as the jailer prepared a magnificent banquet
for his entire household. Or we recline at table with the
poor and lowly, those persons wondrously saved as in

Psalms 22:26–27. We belong by faith to such a cloud of witnesses (Heb 12:1).

Then we recall Jesus' words that "he will prove the world wrong about sin, about justice and about condemnation." We recognize the justice of God, in that his promises are "justly" fulfilled, as fully as God intended and announced. The world, even our own individual, narrow-minded world, is convinced of sin. We had been wrong to limit God's family to those alive with us on earth. We can enjoy the eternal peace of the deceased. And so we "condemn" spontaneously whatever has been holding us back from believing in the mighty power of the Spirit.

When tragedy summons such mighty responses from our heart, we somehow understand these mysterious words of Jesus:

> I tell you the sober truth:
> It is better for you that I go.
> If I fail to go,
> the Paraclete will never come to you,
> while if I go,
> I will send him to you.

Crises then are not so much a test of our personal endurance but the occasion to realize the overwhelming loyalty and love of the Holy Spirit. Because such consolation reaches beyond our understanding, we can never declare ahead of time how much we can endure for the faith out of love for Jesus. The love of Jesus surpasses our ways of measurement. Only by surrendering in faith will God be able to prove "the sober truth" of his infinite care for us.

Prayer:

Jesus, your past goodness is a pledge of your future goodness but never the measure of it. You will always surpass our expectations. Strengthen our faith so that at moments of new trials, we remain faithful and wait for the coming of the Paraclete.

Wednesday—Sixth Week of Easter

Acts 17:15, 22–34; 18:1. Paul's polished but ineffectual speech at Athens.

John 16:12–15. The Spirit of Truth will come and guide you to all truth. He will speak only what he hears and has received from me.

Paul recognized in the Areopagus at Athens the wonderful, even ecstatic beauty of God's creatures, as carved out of marble. The Greeks exulted in the perfect expression of the human form and carved some of the most exquisite statues of male and female as created by God. Further, their temples to Athena and all the deities remain wonders of the world even today. By these statues and architectural achievements the Greeks sought to communicate with others and to commune within themselves about this wonderful mystery of human nature.

John's gospel for today also alludes to the awesome mystery of human life. We receive the Spirit who gradually reveals what we cannot bear to receive all at once right now. This Spirit has absorbed and has actually become the mysterious life uniting the Father and Son in the Holy Trinity. Earlier, on Monday of the Fifth Week of Easter, Jesus had stated that the Father reveals everything to him. This "truth" of all life and hope, which comes from the Father and becomes the Son, now unites them so closely as to become the person of the Holy Spirit. This Spirit receives, like Jesus, the mystery of God's life and desires, and fulfills Jesus' desire of making this truth a part of our own life. Jesus says in today's gospel:

> the Spirit of truth . . .
> will guide you to all truth . . .
> will speak what he hears
> and will announce to you the things to come.
> In doing this he will give glory to me.

While the Greeks identified the mystery of human greatness with the surface beauty of male and female forms, with majestic structures, or with philosophical concepts, John's gospel recognizes the presence of this mystery more deeply at the roots of our being, far beyond our control, even beyond ourselves in the mystery of God's secret life as Father, Son and Spirit. Therefore, what we are to become—the secrets of the things to come—cannot be expressed in statues or philosophical concepts.

Paul endeavored to win over the Greeks to the far more divine mystery in human life when he spoke on the Areopagus. He directed attention to the altar inscribed "To a God Unknown." He went on to say: "What you are thus worshiping in ignorance I intend to make known to you." Paul ended his polished, well-articulated and carefully reasoned speech with an idea that leaped beyond reason and denied the perfection of human nature as it appeared now to the Greeks. He referred to Jesus whom God "has endorsed in the sight of all *by raising him from the dead.*"

At that point, we are told that "some sneered, while others said, 'We must hear from you on this topic some

other time.'" At best he received a polite and conde-
scending smile: maybe we'll have time for you some other
time—maybe not! Yet, one member of the court of the
Areopagus, by name Dionysius, and a woman named
Damaris, and a few others became believers in Jesus.

Christianity then insists that perfection is not a human product, it cannot be achieved by putting our best
efforts to the task, whether individually or communally.
Perfection exists now as a *hope,* a hope so exalted, so demanding, so mysterious, that it can drive a person to
martyrdom—as it did Jesus and eventually Paul—or to
heroic suffering or to contemplative prayer. The Spirit of
truth seeks to unite men and women in the same bond of
love and affection, of equal dignity and respect, that it
can be compared with the bond uniting Father, Son and
Spirit in the Holy Trinity. This hope is beyond what we
can bear to hear right now, it will eventually exert its superhuman expectations, that like Jesus we will pass
through a valley of sorrow and death and yet by this
same hope we will be raised from the dead.

Such perfection then is not a human achievement. It
can be attained only by surrendering to a power, actually
a Person, the Holy Spirit, and then in this total risk of
what we are at present and of what we can become, we
stake everything upon this ineffable "Truth."

Even if this final accomplishment cannot result from
an expenditure of the best human effort, still as Paul
pointed out to the Athenians, it will be seen *in people.*
This "unknown God," worshiped by the Greeks, does
not dwell in statues or sanctuaries. Rather as Paul pointed out, "it is he who gives to all life and breath and everything else. From one stock he made every nation of humankind to dwell on the face of the earth . . . 'for we are
his offspring' [and so] he calls on all men and women ev-

erywhere to reform their lives." Paul's vision of God's wonder resides in people, all sons and daughters of the same God, all sharing the same dignity and all challenged by the same hopes. Only by such bonds of love and forgiveness can we manifest the bond of love within the Holy Trinity and be absorbed within the mystery. Little by little Jesus sends the Spirit to reveal such expectations. Little wonder too that we cannot bear such a message all at once. Yet in possessing the Spirit we have within us the Person of God, the full message of Jesus, the pledge of what we are to become by dying with Jesus and rising with him.

Prayer:

Lord, grant us a heart, humble and docile to receive and be instructed by your Holy Spirit of truth. Make us also strong, even heroic. May we be led by this Spirit as you were through suffering and death. Sustain us by the hope of your holy resurrection.

Thursday—Sixth Week of Easter*

Acts 18:1–8. Paul leaves Athens and comes to Corinth where he meets the couple, Aquila and Priscilla, and joins them in their trade as tentmakers. Preaching on the Sabbath, Paul runs into opposition as well as acceptance.

John 16:16–20. Jesus said: within a short time you will lose sight of me, but soon you will see me again. Your grief will be turned into joy.

*This mass is celebrated when the feast of the Ascension is transferred to the following Sunday.

The Scriptures accept and record the quick transitions which can come into all our lives. Paul left behind the capital city of Athens with its sophisticated audience and proceeded to Corinth. Here he ran into severe opposition from the Jewish people, yet one of the leaders of the synagogue "put his faith in the Lord." More and more gentiles accepted Paul and turned to the Lord Jesus. Paul continued to minister to the Jewish people, but he is definitely moving away from them toward a gentile environment.

Sudden changes also appear in the gospel narrative. Here it is expressed in terms of Jesus' presence, absence and new presence.

As we review all of these movements, from one part of human life to another, we realize that no stage of our existence is permanent. "The world as we know it is passing away" (1 Cor 7:31).

We learn from world history that when a culture or an empire is at its point of highest development and furthest reach, it is usually at the moment of collapse and disintegration. Usually what breaks an empire or collapses a culture is a small, seemingly insignificant force somewhere on the outer edge. In the Old Testament an upstart from a small vassal state overturned the political equilibrium of the Babylonians and Egyptians and created the Persian Empire; his name was Cyrus the Great. Jesus, from an unknown village called Nazareth, so unimportant as never to be mentioned in the Hebrew Scripture, turned into a key figure of world religions. All of us possess such elements of extraordinary change within our lives and circle of friends and work. We should learn to be tolerant and patient, to be humble and docile, able to learn from every aspect of our lives and from everyone within our acquaintance. That person or that event may be announcing our future, the new coming of Jesus into our lives.

We cannot afford to slough off anyone; we cannot look down our nose at any event; we cannot pass by and keep walking with our head in the clouds, unwilling to learn from what is being said and done. In the ancient Scripture, perhaps no person prefigured the ministry and character of Jesus more than the suffering servant in the prophecy of Isaiah. In one of the Servant Songs (49:1-9a) this servant has "the tongue of a disciple," or more literally "the tongue of one who has been taught." Later in the same Song, the servant suffers shame and humiliation. In this way, the servant is able to uphold those who are cast down and insert a new dignity into the lowest moments of human existence. And from this servant Jesus learned peace and the way of his own apostolate.

Not only will we learn the future from people and events seemingly of little or no importance, but from "nowhere" come the dramatic changes in our lives. Furthermore, these transitions usually happen, by surprise. No matter how well we think to be preparing ourselves, we seem to be caught unaware, at least unable to cope with all that happens. Once more the prophet Second Isaiah instructs us; we may have heard the prophecies over and over again. God may have made sure that we were acquainted with them. Yet, God adds: "Suddenly I take action and they come to be" (Is 48:3). Only if we are gracious, yes humble toward the small people and the incidental details of our life, will we be able to handle the moment of dramatic change. Courteous good nature and patient appreciation instill the courage and strength to do the right thing at traumatic moments of change.

Such kindliness and openness prepare us for that "short while" when Jesus disappears from us and returns to us. Our grief at his departure reaches deeply within us, yet our patience enables us to wait upon the Lord. Such waiting renews our strength (Is 40:31); it develops our longing for what is best in life. This waiting upon the Lord also flows from a temperate and thoughtful response to sorrow.

> You will grieve for a time, but your grief will be turned into joy.

Quickly, suddenly, by surprise the Lord will return, again by means of silent events that we could easily pass by unnoticed.

Jesus returned to Paul in such normal ways at Corinth. The apostle met a couple who engaged in the same trade as himself; they were tentmakers. It seems that they were also Jewish Christians like himself. Not only did they keep Paul in contact with his roots, which could seem to have been severed in the difficult turn of events, but they also kept Paul rooted down to earth in the practical, everyday details of secular life. He would work for his living. It is possible that these normal responses prepared Paul for the sudden, dramatic change: "I will turn to the gentiles." Perhaps, in the secular marketplace where everyone equally works for a living, Paul heard the Lord calling him to broaden his ministry and to gather the foreigners into the community of Jesus' disciples.

When our life seems to collapse suddenly, we are not so much humiliated in our defeats and straightened in the seeming absence of Jesus. Rather, we are reduced to a point where we become brothers and sisters to all God's family. At this moment of gracious love, Jesus "in that little while" returns to us.

Prayer:

> Sing to the Lord a *new* song
> > for he has done wondrous deeds
> > —suddenly, from hiding!
> The Lord has made his salvation known,
> > in the sight of everyone.

Friday—Sixth Week of Easter

Acts 18:9–18. Encouraged by the Lord, Paul remains a year and a half at Corinth.

John 16:20–23. After suffering for a little while, Jesus will return and transform pain into joy that no one can take from us. We will then have no further questions to ask.

Because the Bible is the word of God, we often think to ourselves that it will answer all our questions. Yet, today's Gospel indicates that we will have questions on our mind until the second coming of Jesus. "[Only] on that day you will have no questions to ask me." We might expect such a statement from the early parts of the New Testament, say from the gospel of Mark, or still earlier in the Epistle to the Thessalonians. It would not be surprising if the sacred writer of these first New Testament works would reassure us that sooner or later all our questions will be answered, once the gospels take shape and the traditions of the Church are assembled. Yet, we meet the statement in one of the last of the New Testament writings, the gospel of John. Because this gospel could call upon the entire Hebrew Scriptures and also upon the New Testament Scriptures, its author should have had all the answers. Certainly, the Church should not have had

to wait until the second coming of Jesus—an event which
has still not taken place—before all her questioning
would stop.

Further indecisiveness stirs beneath the surface of
today's biblical readings, and this unsteadiness becomes
all the more surprising in view of the opening incident in
Acts. Jesus appeared to Paul, strengthened him and assured Paul: "I am with you." Yet, after this initial promise, serious questions come to mind. Paul is dragged before the Roman proconsul. Then the case is suddenly
dismissed. The Jewish people turn upon a leading man of
the synagogue, Sosthenes, and beat him up. The account
in Acts gives no reason for this violence; instead, it turns
quickly to say that Paul remained "quite a while" at Corinth, most probably a year and a half. Paul's loyalty to
the Mosaic traditions—despite the fact that his fellow
Jews attempted to put him on trial before the Roman
proconsul—shows up clearly in Paul's consecration of
himself with the Nazirite vow (Num 6:1–21). He shaved
his head and would not cut his hair again until the vow is
completed. He would follow strict dietary laws and keep
himself "ceremonially pure." In a very real sense, Paul
again becomes thoroughly a Jew and immerses himself in
some of the strictest of Jewish customs. He then took
leave from Cenchreae, the seaport of Corinth, facing the
east, and began the journey toward Jerusalem.

All kinds of questions come to our mind. Why was
Sosthenes beaten up publicly? Why would Paul continue
living as a fervent Jew, obedient to its strictest rules,
when he was proclaiming the freedom of Jesus' disciples
from these laws and regulations.

Evidently, Jesus' will for Paul was taking a long time
to be clarified and understood in the mind of the apostle.
We are reminded of the example of Jesus about a preg-

nant woman. She will weep and mourn that her time has come. She suffers greatly, all the while unsure about the child—about its sex, facial features, health—about its future which will affect the parents and the entire family. Paul, and in fact we ourselves are all like that pregnant woman, for we possess hopes beyond our comprehension. We are being called to pledge ourselves to other people and to other work, and often enough the future is not clear. At times there are movements of new life which cause us pain and which raise questions.

We have the assurance of Jesus that "your grief will be turned into joy." Although Jesus in one sense can prove this statement from the mystery of the resurrection in his own life, nonetheless, Jesus' glory seems so far remote from us, particularly from us when we are caught in sorrow and darkness, that his resurrection no longer seems to prove anything. And when more questions arise, Jesus' resurrection does not offer us any clear answers— only the strength to live with our questions still longer!

Yet, somehow or other, mysteriously enough but nonetheless beyond all doubt, we sense the presence of Jesus in our lives. Jesus comes to us "one night" in the midst of our darkness, and the force of his presence seems like a vision. He says to us as to Paul: "Do not be afraid. Go on speaking and do not be silenced, for I am with you." The strongest reassurance comes when we are silent, prayerful, immersed in God's holy presence. In such weakness we sense the strength of God deeply within us.

Jesus' presence does not seem to alter the external form of our lives. Paul continued to live as a very devout Jew, even to the point of taking the Nazirite vow and committing himself to dietary laws stricter than those for the ordinary Jewish person. Even when dragged by some of the Jewish people before the Roman proconsul and when another of his friends, Sosthenes, was publicly beaten up, still Paul remained a faithful Jew. We too are not asked to cut all our ties and disassociate ourselves from family and friends. In fact, the presence of Jesus ought to strengthen those bonds and make our loyalty all the more dependable.

Yet, all the while, our hopes continue to grow within us, as a child develops within its mother's womb. Through prayer and patience, through peace and loyalty, we perceive these wonders and possibilities. We live staunchly within the present moment and yet we realize our call toward Jesus that will transform our lives. Our questions now deepen our spirit of faith in Jesus, our willingness to wait and so to renew our strength.

Prayer:

Christ Jesus, you were put to death for our sake, so closely did you unite yourself with us. Help us to remain united with you, as you are with us in our death, so that you may make us worthy of new life.

Saturday—Sixth Week of Easter

Acts 18:23–38. Paul's third missionary journey begins in v. 23. This notice is followed by the account about Apollos who was instructed about Jesus by the couple Priscilla and Aquila.

John 16:23–28. No longer will the disciples ask questions nor will Jesus speak in veiled language. All of Jesus' teaching will be seen in a new, direct and wondrous way.

While the gospel implies an immediate awareness of

the Holy Spirit and a direct communication between ourselves and the heavenly Father, the first reading seems to take a different slant. Acts points out that despite his brilliance, learning and eloquence Apollos had not advanced beyond the teaching of John the Baptist. Apollos was certainly on the way toward being a disciple of Jesus and was a person of tremendous good will. Yet, good will was not enough. In the plan of God, Apollos would be led into the mystery of Jesus through the ministry of the couple Priscilla and Aquila.

It is interesting to note that the wife's name precedes that of her husband, a phenomenon somewhat unusual for the customs of the time and indicative of the strong role of this woman in the Church's ministry. Texts like this one help us to appreciate the attitude of St. Paul toward women and toward the team work of married people in the apostolate of the Church. This couple not only acted as a welcoming committee at Ephesus but also as educators in theology. To dialogue with someone as sharp and knowledgeable as Apollos and to lead him beyond the Hebrew Scriptures and the preaching of John the Baptist meant that the couple were well informed, capable of making distinctions and advancing the discussion, and most of all open to incisive insights from the Holy Spirit.

For Apollos to advance beyond his perception of the Hebrew Scriptures and beyond his loyalty to John the Baptist, it was necessary that he explore the Bible to its outer limit. Like Job it would be necessary that he be impelled by his inquisitive mind and desire for truth, to reach beyond human consolations and accepted wisdom. With pathetic strength Job wrote about this search:

Oh, that I had one to hear my case,

and that my accuser would write out his
  indictment!
Surely, I would wear it on my shoulder
  or put it on me like a diadem;
Of all my steps I should give him an account;
  like a prince I should present myself before
   him.
This is my final plea; let the Almighty answer
  me! (Job 31:35–37).

Apollos had to be ready for the plunge beyond the limits of what he knew and controlled. He had to be compelled like Job to share his luminous and convincing insights—insights all the while that manifested both sturdy control and fragile fear. What Apollos knew, he knew exceptionally well; but he was also convinced that the fulfillment of his desires lay beyond him and required a risk of all of his knowledge. He had to take his case immediately before his maker. He probably felt again like Job when he was discussing that evening with Priscilla and Aquila:

I will take my flesh between my teeth,
  and take my life in my hand (Job 13:14).

Apollos was risking his security, his theological synthesis, and his renown as a self-possessed preacher to be led beyond the borders of his human knowledge and eloquence.

The Spirit could have led Apollos into the mystery of Jesus in the solitude of a desert or in the privacy of his room. Rather that mysterious journey was made under the direction of two superior teachers and interpreters of spirit, Priscilla and Aquila. Evidently the Spirit is received while people share that spirit with one another. A community of faith must be formed in which it becomes evident that *all* are risking their possessions and even their very selves for what the Spirit will reveal. Within the church of Ephesus the Holy Spirit was granted to God's servant Apollos.

Jesus himself exemplified this process of conversion and transformation. He must leave this world in order to send the Holy Spirit. In this repsect there is a good comparison with the risks of leaving behind the tried and true, experienced by Apollos. To ask in Jesus' name is to be one with Jesus' total surrender to the Father. Only in making such a gift of oneself do we realize where we have come from and where we are being led.

> I did indeed come from the Father;
> I came into the world.
> Now I am leaving the world to go to the
> Father.

These two biblical readings then lay out a plan for spiritual direction. More than that, they show the absolute necessity of seeking and receiving advice in a context of total sharing of the Spirit.

Prayer:
Lord, we pray for the courage to pursue the Scriptures and to know them thoroughly. We confess our need for a Priscilla and Aquila to share the Spirit. Then what is veiled in human wisdom and human control will manifest its wondrous, mysterious person, Jesus.

Monday—Seventh Week of Easter

Acts 19:1–8. At Ephesus Paul met twelve disciples who knew only the baptism of John. After being baptized in the name of Jesus and receiving the Holy Spirit, they spoke in tongues and prophesied.

John 16:29–33. Jesus, the disciples declared, was no longer speaking in veiled language. Jesus answered that they will be scattered and he will be alone. Thus they will find peace in Jesus who has overcome the world.

The "plain" language of Jesus' discourse in John's gospel still baffles us. Why will the disciples find peace in Jesus, once they are scattered, each to his own way, and Jesus is left alone? How does such a disintegration of loyalties and friendship convince the disciples that Jesus knows everything and has come from God?

When we read this gospel episode with the selection from Acts, the "plain" language is scrambled still more as the disciples speak in tongues and prophesy. Such an extraordinary manifestation of the Spirit draws us beyond rational discourse and human logic. When God's Spirit descends into our midst in such a marvelous way, we can do only one of two things: either declare it all a hoax and walk away, or acknowledge that God is present, beyond all doubt and beyond all discussion. Earlier in the Acts of the Apostles, when a group of gentiles began to speak in tongues, Peter declared: "What can stop these people who have received the Holy Spirit, even as we have, from being baptized with water?" (Acts 10:47). And when Peter was later challenged that he "entered the house of uncircumcised men and ate with them" (Acts 11:2), his only defense was: "the Holy Spirit came upon them ... Who was I to interfere with him?" (Acts 11:15,17).

Peter's plain speech repudiated even the possibility of discussing his actions. The Church was left with no other option but to accept this wondrous intervention of the Holy Spirit.

Normally, plain speech functions in a different way. It moves with clear ideas and in logical sequence. We are able to obtain further clarification and more nuanced reasons. We can express our difficulties about the logic. If our minds are alert and if we are able to express our ideas clearly, we are in control. Unless logical reasons are presented, we will remain unconvinced and uncommitted. We are free to accept or reject on the logic of the reasoning.

Tongues and prophecy, on the contrary, reach beyond the limits of logic and plain speech. Tongues are an ecstatic expression of the wondrous experience of the Holy Spirit. Tongues reach into foreign languages and beyond—like the many stops of an organ, opened up in full power, as the fingers touch one key after another. The sound is overwhelmingly beautiful, so much so that it drowns out and prohibits the accompanying sound of a singer's words. Communication is more by experience; it happens by touching the strings of emotion and the memory fibers in the heart. Such reactions are not subject to logic; they just happen! And if they happen, one can only say: yes! amen! hallelujah! Praise the Lord! Or as Peter responded: "the Holy Spirit came upon them.... Who was I to interfere" by logic or even by theology? I proceeded at once to baptize them, uncircumcised as they were, different as they were even from the Lord Jesus who was thoroughly a Jew.

Yet, such a response, which rules out all further discussion and certainly all further objections, has the hallmark of plain speech in that it is immediately "yes" or "no," as Jesus wanted our language to be (Matt 5:37). This kind of reply, which waves aside all further discussion and acts at once, possesses another quality of plain speech. Unveiled language, which says it as it is, reaches to the heart or center, and there it discovers the God inspired ability of the human heart to be heroic. Quick reactions can be impulsive; they can also reveal an extraordinary power to love, to protect, to forgive, to die as a martyr.

Jesus' plain speech touches that divinely inspired gift in all of us to act beyond reason (not against reason) and to do what can be explained only afterwards as healthy, beautiful and good. Even though the disciples scattered and left Jesus alone, still Jesus then manifested such strength and resourcefulness, that all will confess: we are not alone; Jesus and the Father are with us. At no time does Jesus' example of forgiving others call us to forgive so heroically as in the story of his Passion. Jesus exemplifies the plain speech of forgiving seventy times seven (Matt 18:22) and of loving to the extent of dying for one's friends (John 15:13).

Jesus' actions bring an immediate response from us: I too must forgive again. I too must be willing to die. I cannot discuss nor negotiate these decisions. The Spirit has moved me. My language reaches beyond rational discourse and I can speak only in tongues. I must fulfill the prophecy of Jesus. Heroic response corresponds to our nature as created and inspired by God.

Prayer:

Lord Jesus, we find our peace in you, even as we suffer with you from the inspirations of the Spirit. We take courage in that you have overcome the world by your extraordinary example. Through your Holy Spirit, we can live at peace with our nature which is meant to be heroic. We thank you for telling us this ennobling truth as plainly as you did.

Tuesday—Seventh Week of Easter

Acts 20:17–27. Speaking at Miletus to the elders of Ephesus, Paul says that he is compelled by the Spirit to go to Jerusalem where he will suffer chains and more hardship. He does so fearlessly, for he has announced the gospel in its entirety.

John 17:1–11. Jesus is to be glorified in this, his hour, for he has finished the work given him to do. Eternal life, then, is to know the one true God and Jesus whom he has sent.

Both Paul and Jesus indicate that an important phase of their ministry has been completed: Paul must proceed to Jerusalem and if he survives the persecutions in that city, he hopes to sail westward to Rome and then to Spain; Jesus declares that he has finished the work given to him by the heavenly Father and now asks: "Do you now, Father, give me glory at your side?"

Paul's words take the form of a final address in which he sums up the duties of pastors and religious leaders. Jesus, on the other hand, prays aloud and offers us one of those rare insights. We are told the content of his prayer to the Father.

Whether in sermon or in prayer, each looks to the future with calm faith and free conscience. Both Paul and Jesus confess from their heart that they have done their very best. Paul states plainly to the elders: "You know how I lived among you from the first day I set foot in the province of Asia—how I served the Lord with humility through the sorrows and trials that came my way from the plottings" of some people. As Jesus prays that the Father give him glory at his side, he adds: "These men you gave me were yours; they have kept your word. I have made your name known to them."

Paul adds many instructions which would be out of place in a prayer that Jesus spoke. We detect a strong confidence and self-assurance. His entire life has been an open book, for he lived, preached and made a secular living to support himself, all in a very visible way. He states so easily what others would be forced to admit: "I put no value on my life if only I can finish my race and complete the service to which I have been assigned by the Lord Jesus." For this reason a stern warning follows: "Therefore I solemnly declare this day that I take the blame for no man's conscience for I have never shrunk from announcing to you God's design in its entirety." Paul's church has been more than adequately instructed: "Never did I shrink from telling you what was for your own good, or from teaching you in public or in private."

Jesus' self-confidence appears much more indirectly: "you have given him [that is, the Son, Jesus himself] authority over all humankind, that he may bestow eternal life on those you gave him." Again, Jesus declares almost by way of gratitude to the Father for the privilege confided to him: "I entrusted to them the message you entrusted to me, and they received it."

Along with this calm interior strength, manifested clearly though differently by Paul and Jesus, each faces a future of uncertainty. Paul does not know the exact details, only that chains and hardships await him at Jerusalem. He admits that he will not see the Ephesians again. According to some scholars, Paul did return to this area. In that case his statement here must be modified with some clause as "insofar as I see the situation right now."

Jesus, for his part, prays for his disciples. Their future is uncertain because of the dangers and tensions, the demands and disappointments of the apostolate. "For these I pray ... I am in the world no more, but these are in the world as I come to you." Jesus could not, or at least did not predict exactly what lies ahead; he would only pray that his followers remain faithful to his person and to his teaching.

Interior strength and a clear conscience do not remove the holy fear and healthy caution about the future. Our previous experience of God does not give us the right or privilege to predict the future, much less to tell God what it ought to be. We are not in a position to quote the Scriptures back to God and insist on the future outcome of our lives! Like Paul, we must be willing to accept the chains and hardships; like Jesus we must pray for enlightenment and strength. We continue to live "in the world," as Jesus said in prayer about his followers. To live in the world means that we must continue to interact with many unpredictable uncertainties, with change of mood and ideas on the part of others.

Yet, we can face the future calmly. For when we finish the work given to us by the Father, God will give us glory at his side.

Prayer:

Blessed are you, O Lord, day by day, for you bear our burden and are our salvation. As we begin each day anew, its joys will resound in your heart and its sorrows weigh upon your shoulders. We look confidently at the uncertainties of our future.

Wednesday—Seventh Week of Easter

Acts 20:28–38. Paul continues his farewell address to the Elders of Ephesus. He sternly warns them to carefully shepherd the flock, to avoid avarice and to be generous. There are moments too of heartfelt prayer and anguish in that they might not see his face again.

John 17:11–19. Jesus' priestly prayer reaches out for God's protection of the disciples who must remain in the world that hated Jesus and will also despise and persecute them.

The necessity of prayer and of concern about his disciples is proven beyond all doubt by the fact that Jesus himself lost one of his own followers, Judas Iscariot, "him who was destined to be lost in fulfillment of the Scripture." The Bible never predicted that a man named Judas Iscariot would betray Jesus and then commit suicide, but it did point out how one's own friends, for good or evil reasons in their own mind, can turn against God. Jeremiah was told by the Lord: "even your own brothers, the members of your father's house, will betray you; they have recruited a force against you" (Jer 12:6). Psalm 69:9 cries aloud: "I have become an outcast to my brothers, a stranger to my mother's sons."

We cannot take the future for granted. We cannot presume that we ourselves will always make the right judgment or courageously act upon a good decision. We cannot take for granted that others will always be acting sincerely, or if they are sincere, that their judgments are well formed and for our good.

At this point the Scriptures do not advise us to be suspicious of everyone. Nor do they seek to draw us out of the world to some solitary spot. As Jesus prayed: "I do not ask you [heavenly Father] to take them out of the world but to guard them from the evil one."

Biblical advice moves in another direction, asking us to look toward our own motives, our prayer and our concern for tradition. True, Paul refers to wolves who will distort the truth and says to be on one's guard against them. Prudence and common sense dictate that we be reasonably cautious and not permit ourselves to be swept along by every wind of an idea! Yet, Paul gives much more attention to other advice.

The elders are to remember Paul's blood and tears, his manual labor and his tireless preaching of the gospel. Strength of conviction and strong emotional ties are revealed in Paul's words: "I never ceased warning you individually even to the point of tears." Paul's solicitude reached to each person individually and it came from a heart flowing over with tears. Paul then speaks of the word which he preached and to which he is confiding the elders at Ephesus. This gospel came from Paul's heart, and the words were soaked with Paul's tears and blood. In a literal sense, he mingled his own tears and blood with those of Jesus, from whose dying side came water and blood (John 19:34). The elders too are to preach with concern for the truth but equally with emotional conviction.

We are to face the future by concern for the poor. After Paul explicitly describes how he worked to support himself and his companions—he did so with "these hands of mine" in an open gesture—he tells the elders to do the same. "I have always pointed out to you that it is by such hard work that you must help the weak." We are to provide for our future by making it even more insecure; we are to give away what little we possess. Such a generous spirit will insure good judgment on our part and will enable us to form good evaluations about others.

Paul then quotes from the Lord Jesus "who said, 'There is more happiness in giving than receiving.' " This precise statement cannot be found in any of the gospels. It is very surprising that Luke who composed one of the gospels as well as the book of Acts did not include it in his collection of Jesus' sayings. Paul must be depending upon an oral tradition and we see how true it is that there would not be "room enough in the entire world to hold the books" if all that Jesus said and did were written down (John 21:24–25). We look toward the future, not only aware of the written Scriptures, but also of the many traditions and customs handed down in our Church. We need to be continually aware of the example of the saints and to look to the "cloud of witnesses" who have preceded us (Heb 12:1).

Despite the difficulties and trials ahead of us in the world, we live joyfully. Jesus advises us in his prayer to the Father: "I say all this while I am still in the world that they may share in my joy completely." Without joy we suspect the worst and are not willing to accept the good in anyone. This joy is deep, it brings tranquility, it bears the fruit of patience. It fits us well to face what the future may bring.

Finally, both Paul and Jesus, each in his own way, state that we have been consecrated by the word or by the truth, by the gospel and by tradition. We are as sacred as the word, we are as much God's creation as the word that comes from his inspiration. We never doubt our relationship with God.

Prayer:

Lord, in today's responsorial psalm, you tell us that

you give power and strength to your people. Let us be your instruments that all the kingdoms of the earth sing your goodness. We look out upon that world and upon our future with your blessing.

Thursday—Seventh Week of Easter

Acts 22:30; 23:6–11. Paul, as he anticipated, was arrested in Jerusalem. The Roman commander summoned him to appear before the Sanhedrin. Paul centered the discussion, which soon degenerated into a violent dispute, around the resurrection. That night in a vision the Lord consoled Paul and called him to be his witness in Rome.

John 17:20–26. Jesus continues his priestly prayer, asking the Father that "all may be one as you, Father, in me, and I in you." All will then see the glory of the Lord.

Jesus signals unity as the most characteristic mark of his disciples, the sign and the goal of true faith. Jesus prayed:

I pray that they [my disciples] may be [one] in us, that the world may believe that you sent me.

Paul of Tarsus appears in today's reading, yet not as a messenger of peace and unity. He deliberately stirred a discussion, which he knew would turn into a shouting match and then into physical abuse. He got the Sadducees pitted against the Pharisees on the subject of the resurrection from the dead. Paul aligned himself with the Pharisees (23:6).

Paul wrote eloquently about peace and unity in 1 Corinthians 11–13 and in Ephesians 4. He was not always stirring up trouble. Jesus for his part was not always a messenger of peace. Jesus had put this question before his disciples:

> Do you think that I have come to establish
>   peace on the earth?
> I assure you, the contrary is true; I have come
>   for division.
> From now on, a household of five will be
>   divided
> three against two and two against three;
> father will be split against son and son against
>   father,
> mother against daughter and daughter against
>   mother
> ... (Luke 12:51–53).

Although unity and peace remain a sign of Jesus' discipleship, nonetheless, Jesus was not giving in to peace at any price! Certainly Jesus wanted his followers to display patience and forebearance, to know when and how to be silent, yes even to turn the other cheek (Luke 6:29). But Jesus also called for courage (if a hand scandalize you, cut it off!—Mark 9:43–48), for truth (let your language be yea or nay—Matthew 5:37), for generosity (the one line which Paul quotes of Jesus in Acts reads, "There is more happiness in giving than receiving"—Wed, 7th Week), for fidelity, as his statement on marriage and divorce makes clear, for total dedication ("let the dead bury the dead"—Luke 9:60).

Jesus' disciples were not united around the weak principle that no body will ever hurt the feelings of anyone else, but rather around an intense desire to enable one another to seek and share the best. Jesus stirred his followers to see a vision of goodness, of kindliness, of peace and justice, of fidelity and honesty. This vision beckoned at times to overwhelming happiness, at other times to the cross and the loss of all that one holds dear.

More than anything else according to the gospel for today, this unity was to be modeled upon that of the Holy Trinity. Here the Father shares his entire life with the Son, and the two are locked in love so intense that it becomes the person of the Holy Spirit. For this goal to be realized, Jesus' disciples must fix their eyes upon him, who in turn lives only for the Father in the bond of the Holy Spirit. Jesus in turn will share with his disciples the glory given to him by the Father before the world began. Jesus also declared:

> Your love for me may live in them,
> and I may live in them.

The resurrection then became all important. The resurrection had enabled Jesus even to despise this earthly life out of love for others and to die for them. In that case he would share the ultimate moment of human existence but he would also be able to introduce the eternal life of God into human death. His own resurrection became a harbinger of everyone's resurrection. Because each of us sees this vision of Jesus in glory, we too are strengthened to give our lives for others. We are able to undergo heroic suffering for the sake of those we love—and this object of love may have been a stranger up till that moment.

Paul, therefore, could not compromise on the resurrection. Unity was not worth such a cost! Therefore, he clearly announced: "I am a Pharisee and was born a Pharisee. I find myself on trial now because of my hope in the resurrection of the dead." Paul sought unity, in this case with the Pharisees, unity that kept a vision of the highest hopes before others.

At the same time Paul's words manifest an uncanny prudence. He averted the attack from his own person by pitting Pharisees and Sadducees against one another. Both were opposed to Paul for declaring that Jesus was the promised Messiah. A person, therefore, does not throw caution to the winds in order to rally round the banner of reckless courage. Just as weakness is not worth the cost and is to be despised, neither is imprudence to be advised, even if it comes under the name of bravery.

Jesus unites his disciples around the very best of human qualities. Jesus' ideals do more than sanctify our talents of mind and body. Jesus puts a vision before us that leads us beyond what we consider possible. Jesus does more that that. He places that desire at our heart in the person of himself. He said:

> I living in them, you [Father] living in me—
> that their unity may be complete.

Prayer:

Lord, I set you ever before me. My heart is glad and my soul rejoices. My body too abides in confidence. You show me the path to life, fullness of joy in your presence. You grant this vision to all my brothers and sisters and we are united in the best of ourselves. Not even death can destroy this hope and you will not permit your faithful one to undergo corruption. Your resurrection is our hope, the reward of our unity.

Friday—Seventh Week of Easter

Acts 25:13–21. The new Roman governor, Festus, explains to his guests King Agrippa and Bernice that the case of Paul the prisoner is on the docket, awaiting Paul's transfer to the emperor's court in Rome.

John 21:15–19. Jesus thrice asks Peter: "Do you love me?" and three times Jesus receives Peter's attestation that he certainly does. Jesus then announces how Peter in his old age will be bound and led away. Finally, at the end Jesus said, "Follow me."

The sequence of events is important, so natural and yet so filled with spiritual meaning that we must delay here. Youth is marked by an active pursuit of goals. Many options open out before a young man or young woman. With study, experimentation and advice they freely decide. As a person gets older, a more passive acceptance of the inevitable seems to be the only option. As we become still older and now helpless, we may be able to do nothing at all but *wait* for the inevitable. As we long for death and its release from misery, we must wait for the moment that God decides. At the very end Jesus says, "Follow me!"

In the more active span of life, with many good possibilities opening out before us, we also fail at times to choose what is best. We may turn to evil. Such at least happened to the apostle Peter. Three times out of fear he denied Jesus (Mark 14:66–72). After the resurrection when the apostles had returned to their former trade of fishing, seemingly because their vision of Jesus had evaporated in his death, Jesus appeared to them. He singled out Peter and three times asked, "Do you love me?" Peter no longer seems to be the ebullient impulsive man of the earlier days. He has been humiliated, he has failed even to the extent of betraying Jesus, he has returned to the only occupation which he could manage. Peter is ready to enter the next stage of his life.

Peter has been sobered by failure. He has been made compassionate by his own need for forgiveness and mercy. His heart is open to more and more people, for he shares their reactions and feelings. Not once, not even twice, but three times Jesus asks and insists, "Do you love me?" When Peter answers with humble love, with total surrender ("Lord, you know everything"), then Jesus commissions him to "Feed my sheep."

In this second stage of his career, Peter summons his first energy and moves from Jerusalem to Antioch and then to Rome. Love, humility, compunction and obedience to the Lord are to be the hallmarks of his ministry. As such, he is the rock of the Church and head of the apostolic band. Even though Peter acts with all his power, still there is a quality of passivity about that exercise: to love and to be loved, to be humble and open to others in their ideas and talents, to be sorrowful for sin and able to appreciate the weakness of others, to obey Jesus at all costs.

Jesus not only singled out Peter from all the apostles but called him particularly to "Feed my sheep." He was to be the supreme pastor of the Church. Jesus, however, did more. He also announced the martyrdom of Peter:

> When you are older
> you will stretch out your hands,
> and another will tie you fast
> and carry you off against your will.

In the third stage of Peter's life, the quality of being passive to God's will and to the desires of others will be all the more pronounced. Peter will be helpless! And at that point, Jesus adds, "Follow me." Just as Jesus' supreme act of obedience to his heavenly Father happened when he accepted the cross and allowed others to take his life from him, Peter too would summon all his power and make the most energetic response of his entire life by passively accepting death. "Against his will" and yet willingly because it was the Father's will, Peter allowed himself to be led away. His only request, according to tradition was to be crucified upside down. He was unworthy to die exactly as did the Lord Jesus!

We too pass through these natural stages of life. We may think that our most valuable contribution comes when we are young. Then we bounce with life and vigor; then we choose between a thousand and one possibilities, in order to do the very best for God. We seem to make all kinds of sacrifices, putting aside many options, for what we believe is what God wants. Yet, there can be a great deal of selfishness in all this, certainly more than a little forgetfulness about others. We just have not lived long enough to really know how they feel. How can the healthy who have never been sick know how physical weakness corrodes a person's interest, desires and patience. The young in this first stage of their existence can be too innocent or too impulsive, to be tolerant of weakness in others. Sooner or later, they enter the second stage, usually because of some traumatic experience. Peter's dramatic change came with his betrayal of Jesus just as the Master was humiliated, rejected and killed.

The second stage can become monotonous, as fewer and fewer options appear on the horizon and we settle down more seriously to do the one important task of our life. Yet, once we have experienced how to do it capably well, our energy begins to seep away through sickness and age. This is the moment when we repeat the maxim: if age only could and youth only would.

The third and last stage is our final illness and death. Again Jesus repeats the beckoning of our first call. He says once more, "Follow me." How can we, as we are unable to walk and to do anything that seems productive? We simply wait. Yet, from deep in our soul we know the meaning of love. Love gives not things but oneself. Love does not seek gifts, even great opportunities, only the person of the other. Jesus does not have to ask: "Do you love me?" He knows it and we know it. He says simply, "Follow me!" We respond with our entire self, most lovingly, most actively for we are not distracted by any other option or choice, most passively for we are carried off. The Scripture says, "against your will," yet that means how much we would want to run, not be carried. "Against your will" is the ultimate gift of our entire self to Jesus.

Prayer:

Lord, allow me now and always to join in the prayer of the psalmist, "Bless the Lord ... *all my being!*" Turn each day of my life into an opportunity to offer a new part of myself to you. Make this offering, in response to your request, a blessing and a manifestation of your goodness in my life.

Saturday—Seventh Week of Easter

Acts 28:16–20, 30–31. Paul was under house arrest at
Rome, till his case ran out in two years and he was ac-
quitted. He assures the Jewish elders at Rome that "I
wear these chains solely because I share [with you] the
hope of Israel."

John 21:20–25. Jesus assured the disciple whom he loved:
"You will stay until I come." To Peter he said: "Your
business is to follow me." The gospel then ends, admitting that the world's books could not contain all the
details of Jesus' words and actions.

The readings for this day are drawn from the final
verses of Acts and of John's gospel. Acts rounds out the
total theological purpose of St. Luke, which extended
from his earlier book, the gospel, into his second book,
called *The Acts of the Apostles.* Luke's gospel moves from
Old Testament Jerusalem (Chs. 1–2) or from the Jordan
River where the conquest of the Promised Land once began under Joshua (Ch. 3), full circle back again to Jerusalem, where Jesus was crucified and glorified and where
the disciples are back again in the temple, praising God
(Chs. 22–24). One of the central features in Luke's gospel
is found in the "Journey Narrative" (Lk 9:51; 19:28) during which Jesus' entire ministry is put in the context of
going up to Jerusalem, as a way toward the cross and glorification.

Acts too begins in Jerusalem. Its central action consists in Paul's "Journey Narrative" (Chs. 13–28). Paul
travels through the Greek speaking world several times,
founding churches, almost always by way of bringing the
synagogue and its Jewish worshipers (or many of them at
least) into the Christian community. All of Paul's activity
leads up to Rome, where the hope of Israel triumphs in a

world manifestation of the Lord. Rome, then, is the new Jerusalem where the disciples praise the Lord. Here too is the sign of the cross in the suffering and martyrdom of the saints (Paul, however, at this time was to be set free) and here also is fulfillment of centuries of waiting and prediction.

The "Journey Narrative" of Luke's gospel and of Acts must find a path in our lives. It must work its way to the center. Every other moment and every other experience, good or bad, easy or difficult, is pointed toward this new "Jerusalem," this "Rome." Here we praise God for his wonderful acts in our lives. Prophecies are fulfilled. At this point the words of Jesus to the beloved disciple come to mind: "I want him to stay until I come." As Jesus explained to Peter, this statement does not mean that we will never die but rather Jesus will come to get us. Jesus comes at the final fulfillment of all prophecies in our lives.

Both the gospel and Acts then inflame our faith and confidence. No moment is to be considered lost and useless. All can be turned into the direction of Jerusalem. That road has all kinds of stops or stages along its route. There are stages of triumph and joy; others of strenuous effort; still others of blunder and error. At times we have to go around a barrier, and then for a while we are going backward. There is the necessity of resting and recouping strength. All of these moments are found in the gospel and in Acts. Jesus can turn each experience—no matter what it may have been—into a new turn in the road toward our destination, the heavenly Jerusalem.

If the final stage along the way turns out to be Rome, the counterpart to the earthly Jerusalem, then all experiences point toward Rome, Rome is always the rallying center for all God's disciples. Here is where the unity which Jesus desired earnestly for his Church is typified (see Thursday, Seventh Week of Easter). At the end, then, we reassemble with all our family, community and friends. Even those persons who parted company through disagreement and quarrels will find their way to this destination for everyone. One of the final stages along the way to Rome—Jerusalem, then, must be the place of reconciliation.

The final verses in John's gospel, however, seem to give a slightly different nuance to the sense of arrival at the end, to this fulfillment of prophecy in our lives, and to this coming of the Lord Jesus for us. "The world," John writes at the very end, "does not have space to hold the books to record" all the details of Jesus' life and ministry. We get the sense of much more to learn and to experience. The end, in a true sense, is only the beginning. What we have seen and heard about Jesus, as we follow along the route with him to our Jerusalem-Rome, stores up memories that need an eternity of time to unravel. Every other person must feel the same.

"I want him to stay until I come"—Jesus' statement about John and now about ourselves—can have an extended meaning. "Wait!" I come anew each moment of eternity. I come to revive your memories. I come to share the memories of all your brothers and sisters. "Wait until I come." Eternity will be the continuation of the final moment in our earthly Jerusalem-Rome. Jesus comes wondrously—and he comes again and again. Even as we meditate now on the gospels for our consolation, in heaven these and thousands of other memories—too many for the world to contain the books—will be reexperienced. Our prayer now is a foretaste of that heavenly joy. What

Paul said to his Jewish visitors in Rome, he says to us: we share the hope of Israel, as fulfilled in the death and resurrection of Jesus at Jerusalem.

Prayer:

Lord, you promise that "the just will gaze on your face." We believe that each step along our way of life enables us to see the face of Jesus for we are experiencing moments of his earthly life. Continue this faith in us, until we see you, face to face, in the heavenly Jerusalem.

PART TWO

Sundays and Feastdays
of the
Easter Season

Easter Sunday—(A-B-C Cycles)

Acts 10:34, 37–43. The first reading for Easter draws its material from Peter's Pentecost discourse at Jerusalem: the apostles were witnesses that Jesus was raised from the dead. Jesus commissioned them to preach that he is the one about whom the prophets testified.

Col 3:1–4. Your life is hidden with Christ in God. When Christ our life appears, then you shall appear with him in glory.

1 Cor 5:6–8*. Let us celebrate the feast not with the old yeast, which we are to cast out, but with the unleavened bread of sincerity and truth.

John 20:1–9. Peter and John, being informed by Mary Magdalene that the stone had been rolled away from the tomb, ran to the garden where Jesus was buried. "As yet they did not understand the Scripture that Jesus had to rise from the dead."

Easter is the glorious finale of Hebrew prophecy and of Jesus' earthly life. As Peter preached in his Pentecost sermon, his very first after the resurrection: "To him all the prophets testify, saying that everyone who believes in him has forgiveness of sins through his name." Without the resurrection, Jesus' life would have been a total failure, all the more disappointing for it had promised so much. With the resurrection, every moment of Jesus' ministry takes on significant meaning. Even today we are still looking to the gospels for direction and inspiration; their words are never exhausted.

The resurrection was the keystone, that central rock without which the entire archway would collapse; the Spirit of Pentecost, sent to us by the risen Jesus, is the

*Alternate second reading.

wisdom and strength to see how every part fits together in the archway.

Despite this crucial role of the resurrection, today's scriptural readings do not give a sense of final fulfillment, nor a feeling of absolute security. Despite his enthusiasm while preaching on Pentecost, Peter is simply inaugurating the mission of the Church to bring the gospel of Jesus to the world. Over 1900 years later we are still going about that task.

Paul's epistle to the Colossians has exalted moments. "You have been raised up in company with Christ." Yet, Paul changes his style to that of exhortation and veiled warning: "Set your heart on what pertains to higher realms. . . . Be intent on things above rather than things of earth. After all, you have died!" In writing to the Corinthians, Paul is much less ebullient. Here he can even become sarcastic, as in Chapter One when he praises them for every virtue except the important one of charity, or in 2 Corinthians 10 when he defends himself against the slurs and lies of jealous Christians! Paul, therefore, writes seriously: "Get rid of the old yeast. . . . Let us celebrate the feast not with the old yeast." Paul indicates that some bad yeast is raising sinful or evil reactions among the people.

Finally, John's gospel leaves us guessing. It ends with the remark that the apostles, Peter and the other disciple whom Jesus loved, "did not understand the Scripture that Jesus had to rise from the dead." Even though the women rush to announce that the stone had been rolled away and the tomb was empty, the apostles would not accept the conclusion, so obvious to us, that Jesus must have risen from the dead.

All these sorts of reactions happen in our own lives. It takes wonderful news a long time to seep into our consciousness and still a longer time to convince us beyond all doubt that Jesus has risen from the dead and that we share in that glory. At times we harbor some "bad yeast" at the heart of our lives: some prejudice, some hurts, some serious disappointments, an inferiority complex, some bad habits. We are unwilling to cast out this bad yeast which provokes evil responses in us.

If we take seriously Paul's charge, "Set your heart on what pertains to higher realms," we may have to disengage ourselves from some unnecessary, frivolous or even scandalous pleasures. We may have to relocate our sense of values. We may have to dampen our ambition for wealth, prestige and financial security. We may have to open our family or community to some sick or incapacitated people who need attention and require expensive medicine. To "set our hearts on what pertains to higher realms," might actually expect us to look more immediately to persons of our family, relations and neighborhood, badly crying out for help in their loneliness or abandoned state. Yet, such attention to these people reduces our time and finances for personal pleasure.

To "understand the Scriptures" we must be people of great hope, in ourselves and in others. We need to be optimistic about church and country. Then when someone else, like the women in today's gospel, brings good news, we will immediately believe. We will not be like the apostles, even the chosen ones like Peter and the disciple whom Jesus loved, who ran to the tomb to check out the report of the women, and still remained baffled in their unbelief. They were ready to believe anything but good news!

Easter, then, is the beginning of attitudes and spirit, of hopes and ambition, of confidence and trust. It is our responsibility to cooperate with this wonderful grace that

Jesus is offering to us. We will move ahead with determination to new possibilities, as the apostles eventually did after Pentecost; to rid ourselves of bad yeast and evil conditions at the heart of ourselves; to encourage and approve good news.

Prayer:

This day, O Lord, is yours! You have made it in a very special way. It holds particular graces, which lead us to exclaim: "Your mercy endures forever!" Turn our empty tombs into signs of hope and new life. In your company let us seek the things of heaven, already here on earth, in ourselves and in others.

Second Sunday of Easter—"A" Cycle

Acts 2:42–47. A portrayal of the first Christian community at Jerusalem. The disciples held their property and goods in common, worshiped together at the temple, and broke the bread of the Eucharist in the privacy of their home.

1 Pet 1:3–9. This early hymn celebrates new birth in the sacrament of baptism. A Christian can expect not only to relive Jesus' sorrows but also to share in the supreme hope of Jesus' glorious appearance.

John 20:10–30. Jesus confers upon the apostles the power of the Holy Spirit to forgive sins. He also overcomes Thomas' unbelief by beckoning him to examine the marks of the nails and spear on his body.

Much of the First Letter of Peter reflects a baptismal instruction and ceremony of the very early Church. Today's passage would have been the opening hymn of the ritual. It celebrates the new birth of the baptized person, who draws life from the resurrection of Jesus, partakes of eternal life, and possesses an imperishable inheritance.

Not only does the Church exult with hymnic praise over this gift of new life, but the community realizes as well the cost of this life in terms of the death of Jesus which the newly baptized person will also experience. "You may ... have to suffer the distress of many trials." The Christian life inaugurated at baptism, passes repeatedly through the cycle of death to new life.

We think of Paul's theology of baptism in his letter to the Romans:

> Are you not aware that we who were baptized into Christ Jesus were baptized into his death? Through baptism into his death we were buried with him, so that, just as Christ was raised from the dead by the glory of the Father, we too might live a new life (Rom 6:3–4).

Deeply imbedded in the consciousness of the Church then was the faith that life is a sharing in Jesus' resurrection, a life which blossomed from Jesus' obedient and heroic love on the cross. The gift of life in the Church then flows from the cross of Jesus. Peter also wrote in his first epistle:

> Realize that you were delivered from the futile way of life your ancestors handed on to you, not by any diminishable sum of silver or gold, but by Christ's blood beyond all price: the blood of a spotless, unblemished lamb (1 Pet 1:18–19).

Even if the sequence was from cross to resurrection for Jesus, for the newly baptized (or shall we say, the newly born) Christian, it was first a sharing in Jesus' resurrected life and then a participation in his cross. The love and beauty of the new life was bound to bring its suffering and difficulties. Yet each new suffering would lead to a new experience of Jesus' resurrection.

At first, then, the newly born, baptized person experiences love and gentleness within the family of the Church. The Acts of the Apostles describes this idyllic scene. "The community of believers were of one heart and one mind. None of them claimed anything as their own; rather, everything was held in common" (4:32). A spirit of prayer spread over the group, whether at home or in the temple (2:42, 46). They were continually "praising God and winning the approval of all the people" (2:47).

Such family love led to ever greater demands of generosity and forgiveness. And soon we read in the Acts of the Apostles that jealousy, bias, lies, greed and still other faults marred the peace of the community. We remember Ananias and Sapphira, struck dead by God because of their conspiracy and greed (Acts 5:1–11). These faults were all the more serious, because they seemed to deny the meaning of Jesus' resurrection. The Lord, according to their faith, has risen to new life, was sharing that glory with his disciples, and was expected to return any moment to reward the faith and hope of the Church.

Baptism then within a family, community or church of exceptional fervor puts still greater demand upon everyone. Such expectations are never achieved easily, only through much mutual suffering, patience, forgiveness and charity. "They ... shared all things in common" (2:44). Each member of the community must bear the marks of the crucified Jesus.

John's gospel insists that the newly baptized ought to discover those signs of Jesus within the Christians themselves. Even though the gospel recounts an episode about Thomas in the week after the resurrection, still its thrust is toward the Church in the years after the resurrection. Jesus' concluding remark makes this fact very clear:

> Blessed are they who have not seen me
> and have believed.

Faith then that Jesus lives in the community and shares the power of death and resurrection with the Church enables the newly baptized person to endure sorrows and disappointments. When confronted with human weakness and other serious threats and sorrows, the Christian ought to believe that they are seeing the sign of Jesus' scars. With Thomas then they can exclaim, "My Lord and my God." They have been able to believe ever more fully the meaning of their baptism because they can probe the nailprints in Jesus' hands and put their finger into the nailmarks and their hand into his side.

The glory of the resurrection is to be revealed through the weakness of human flesh. The hopes deeply imbedded within the baptized person somehow accentuate these sorrows and disappointments, because hopes reach beyond reality and expect much more than what is seen and what seems possible. Yet, as these hopes remain intact, they show the strength of Jesus' life and resurrection. They bring the Christian through death to new glory and wonder.

Prayer:

Lord, your Church rests upon a cornerstone that has been rejected. Our baptism rests upon your death. Yet, this cornerstone supports a temple of prayer and family where everything is held in common. We realize the cost of such joyful life. Help us always to be strong in suffering the hopes of our baptism and so to see your wondrous life in an every renewed Church.

Second Sunday of Easter—"B" Cycle

Acts 4:32–35. Another summary about the way of life followed by the Jerusalem community, this one emphasizing that all goods were held in common.

1 John 5:1–6. The love of God for us, our obedience toward his commandments, and our faith in Jesus Christ who came through water and blood.

John 20:19–31. Jesus confers upon the apostles the power of the Holy Spirit to forgive sins. He also overcomes Thomas' unbelief by beckoning him to examine the marks of the nails and spear on his body.

The narrative in Acts makes our Christian way seem very simple. We sense a spirit of trust, an attitude of lightheartedness, of sharing everything in common as one family. Whenever such is the case, we know that people have worked hard to achieve this harmony. Some have suffered, others have prayed long to come to this resolve, still others have had to work their way through many personal or societal difficulties. Every family and relationship that is characterized with peace, contentment and simplicity have paid the price, willingly and dearly.

In order that we may receive the grace to be instruments of peace, Jesus has offered much more than gold or silver. He laid down his life. In the second reading, the disciple John begins to unravel the explanation which leads to the cross of Jesus. "Everyone," he wrote, "begotten of God conquers the world." Peace and simplicity are not this world's gifts; rather, they are achieved despite the world which stirs jealousy, fear or excessive desires and unrest. The ability to conquer the world comes from "this faith of ours." Faith here is more than a vague trust in God who will do everything while we sit and wait.

> "Faith," for John, leads to Jesus on the cross.
> Who, then is conqueror of the world?
> The one who believes that Jesus is the
> Son of God.
> Jesus Christ it is who came through
> water and blood—
> not in water only,
> but in water and in blood.

Both here as well as in his gospel (John 19:34–35) the disciple whom Jesus loved adds a strengthening remark: "It is the Spirit who testifies to this, and the Spirit is truth," and again: "this testimony is given by an eyewitness, and his testimony is true. He tells what he knows is true, so that you may believe." The seriousness of this statement is evident.

Jesus' testimony is given "in water and in blood." The immediate reference is to the scene on Golgotha. When the soldier came to break the bones of the three crucified men, Jesus was already dead. A lance was thrust through Jesus' side "and immediately blood and water flowed out." Typically, John is again writing a "sacramental" gospel; he is continually relating events in Jesus' life and death with the sacraments of the Church, particularly with baptism and the Eucharist. This fact becomes more evident when John proceeds to quote the Old Testament account of the paschal lamb. That ceremony forms a link with the paschal meal of the Eucharist.

"Water" symbolizes entrance into the Church

through baptism; "blood," the strength of life, imparted through the Eucharist. These two sacraments play an important part in the early chapters of Acts. The apostles preach and baptize. Those who have been baptized gather for the breaking of bread, as we read last Sunday from Acts (2:42–47). For the community to be gathered together this peacefully, Jesus underwent an excruciating death. He conquered the world from the cross. There he struggled with violence and overcame it. There he destroyed selfishness and false ambition, as he laid down his life and seemingly lost all future hopes for this earth.

Yet, Jesus in overcoming the world from the cross, did more than meet violence with violence. He forgave his enemies for they did not really know what they were doing (*cf.*, Luke 23:34). And so on Easter night, when he returned to the apostles, he conferred upon them the power to forgive in his name. Within that same context we read in today's gospel about Thomas' daring request: "I'll never believe without probing the nailprints in his hands, without putting my finger in the nailmarks and my hand into his side." Forgiveness must face another challenge of effrontery and disbelief, Jesus was ready. He appeared again and invited Thomas to probe the scars of the nails and spear upon his body.

Forgiveness within the new Christian community ranked among the most necessary virtues. Some of the new converts had shouted for the death of Jesus, just a few weeks previously. Others took part in the proceedings of the Sanhedrin. Still others had to face the puzzlement and then the isolation of their family and friends. Peace always presumes a heavy dose of forgiveness!

During these peaceful, happy days of the Easter season we need to be reminded of the price paid by Jesus, by our ancestors in the faith, by our immediate family, relations and community. It is also necessary to celebrate this strong, even heroic tradition—of suffering for the faith and of patient forgiveness—by the sacraments of baptism and the Eucharist. These sacraments in turn must always be seen in relation not only to Jesus' death but also to the suffering and forgiveness undertaken for us by our family and friends.

Prayer:

We can be hard pressed and falling, O Lord, but you help us. You are our strength and our courage. Because of you there is a joyful shout of victory and of peace. You have overcome all obstacles by your share in our suffering. You lead us home.

Second Sunday of Easter—"C" Cycle

Acts 5: 12–16. A third portrait (see "A" and "B" Cycles for the other two) describing the life of the early Jerusalem church. The power of healing is prominent in this account.

Rev 1: 9–11, 12–13, 17–19. John is called to write down his visions by Christ, the Son of Man, once dead and now alive. John shares in the distress, endurance and hopes of his readers.

John 20:19–31. Jesus confers upon the apostles the power of the Holy Spirit to forgive sins. He also overcomes Thomas' unbelief by beckoning him to examine the marks of the nails and spear on his body.

The picture of the Jerusalem church in the early chapters of Acts, especially within the summaries read on the three cycles of the Second Sunday of Easter, glows with peace, quiet enthusiasm and fervent prayer. Each of the three summaries highlights a particular feature: the first (2:42–47), a dedication to prayer; the second (4:32–35), a generous sharing of material goods; this third and final vignette in today's liturgy, an exceptional gift for healing physical illness. The Jerusalem disciples, moreover, felt themselves in full communion with their neighbors and with them went to the temple and performed the full Jewish ritual. They were different in that they expected the second coming of Jesus any moment, at least within their lifetime.

The scene shifts dramatically when we read the book of Revelation. At once we are conscious of a Church, hounded by Roman persecutors and beset with internal problems. The church at Ephesus has "turned aside from your early love" (Rev 2:4); the church at Laodicea is "neither hot nor cold. How I wish that you were one or the other—hot or cold! ... You are lukewarm ... I will spew you out of my mouth!" First fervor then has been dissipated, religion has become routine, some serious moral faults have surfaced.

Just as the sufferings and death of Jesus resulted from political maneuvering and jealousy within the ranks of Jewish leaders, John, the author of Revelation, sees the need of new suffering and purification for the Church during the last decade of the first Christian century. So soon, in fact within fifty to sixty years, the Church was in need of serious reform. Actually, we read that greed and distrust struck early within the Church, already within Chapters 5 and 6 of Acts. Ananias and Sapphira were lying about their finances; Greek speaking Christians felt mistreated by Hebrew speaking Christians! Almost concomitantly a violent storm swirled around the Church. Some of the apostles were imprisoned and scourged, and with the martyrdom of Stephen the "day saw the begin-

ning of a great persecution of the Church at Jerusalem"
(Acts 8:1).

Neither the Church at large, nor anyone of us individually, knows how to deal with prosperity over a long,
and sometimes over a short period of time. The more we
have, the more jealous and defensive we become. Petty
faults evolve into more serious crimes as we begin to lie
to one another, to cheat, to become sensual and pleasure-
loving.

Not only do we begin to degenerate from our first
fervor and strong sense of right and wrong, but we do not
have the ability or strength to reform ourselves. It seems
a truism that no person and no institution contain the
power or wisdom to correct themselves. At least the initial thrust toward reform and purification must come
from the outside. Such, anyway, is the lesson learned
from Acts and from Revelation, two books standing at
the beginning and at the end of the apostolic Church.

This combination of pain and glory, of persecution
and purfication, becomes a pattern of early Church history. Jesus himself reflects this fact when he appears to his
disciples between Easter and Pentecost. He comes in glory, but bearing the marks of the nails and spear upon his
body. Not even in the moment of exultant triumph will
Jesus allow his followers to forget the cross. That memory is most necessary to interpret the meaning of suffering
and persecution in the days ahead.

Yet, the harried and at times tumultuous situation of
a Church under strain and persecution is not meant to
last. It is only a very necessary but passing stretch of
time. We are meant to be peaceful and tranquil, trusting
and trusted. The power of healing the sick is prominent
in the early Church. Sickness too is only a stage along the

way. Normally God wants us to contribute our talents, even our physical strength to the community. Yet we need the sick and disabled, just as we need the marks of the nails and spear on the body of Jesus. In this way we appreciate the origin and purpose of good health.

The presence of the aged, the sick and the handicapped turns into an appearance of the Lord Jesus, who says to us:

> Peace be with you!
> Take your finger and examine my hands.
> Put your hand into my side.
> Do not persist in your unbelief,
>   but believe!

If we respond to the disabled or helpless members of our community with the tender concern with which Thomas touched Jesus, then we will learn to say in our hearts:

> My Lord and my God!

And Jesus will urge us to be quicker in our response to the needy and to see at once his presence in them:

> You became a believer because you saw me.
>   Blest are they who have not seen and
>   have believed.

The persecutors too can be transformed as the violent Saul of Tarsus into the apostle St. Paul, as was the pagan Roman empire into the Christian state. The energy of the persecutor contains overwhelming power to follow through on a purpose and to be obsessed with an ideal.

Persecutors are not lukewarm, nor have they fallen from their first love, as happened in the early Church according to the writer of Revelation.

The Church spans the centuries of fervor and decline, of peace and persecution, through the continual presence of Jesus: "I am the First and the Last and the One who lives. I was dead but now I live forever and ever. I hold the keys of death and the nether world."

Prayer:

Jesus, you repeated to your disciples and now to us the mysterious statement of the ancient Scriptures: "The stone which the builders rejected has become the cornerstone." Enable us to see in our own suffering, in our poor and handicapped neighbors, in our persecutions and trials, "The stone . . . rejected." This stone is *you*; it is our way to purification and new life.

Third Sunday of Easter—"A"Cycle

Acts 2:14, 22–28. On Pentecost, Peter stated that Jesus was handed over to death "by the set purpose and plan of God" and therefore could not be bound by death's bitter pangs." He was shown "the paths of life."

1 Pet 1:17–21. We have been redeemed not "by silver or gold but by Christ's blood beyond all price." "Your faith and hope, then, are centered in God."

Luke 24:13–35. The account of the two men on their way to Emmaus.

Both Peter's statements in the first major address of his apostolic career, as well as Jesus' remarks to the three men on the way to Emmaus, clearly accentuate the fact that the Messiah must suffer. His suffering and death were "by the set purpose and plan of God." Jesus' words were even more insistent as he spoke on Easter afternoon to the two men on the road to Emmaus. "Did not the Messiah have to undergo all this so as to enter into his glory?" Jesus then interpreted "every passage of Scripture which referred to him," "beginning ... with Moses and all the prophets," that the Messiah must suffer. Jesus was to repeat this same idea when he appeared later the same day to the Eleven (Luke 24:46).

Evidently, the Scriptures were not all that clear, if they needed to be interpreted. A reader can always pick and choose and possibly miss what is crucial. More than that, however, the sacred writings also needed the example of Jesus to show what they really meant. Without that example they might seem to be just theory, or confusing possibility, or unacceptable happenings. Therefore, the death and resurrection of Jesus needed the ancient Scriptures to see a large plan, stretching through the ages and directed to this moment by God. The Scriptures needed the death and resurrection of Jesus to prove that God really meant some of his words!

Most difficult of all to accept, perhaps, is the continuous biblical faith in God's immediate presence. God is closer than we are to ourselves. Such is the ecstatic praise of the psalmist:

O Lord, you have probed me and know me;
You know when I sit and when I stand;
you understand my thoughts from afar. . . .
Even before a word is on my tongue,
    behold, O Lord, you know the whole of it.
Behind me and before, you hem me in
    and rest your hand upon me. . . .
If I go up to the heavens, you are there,

if I sink to the nether world, you are
    present there. . .
If I say, "Surely the darkness shall hide me,
    and night shall be my light."
For you darkness itself is not dark,
    and night shines as the day
                            (Ps 139:1–2, 4–5, 8, 11–12).

The psalmist hints at God's presence in darkness, a
biblical image of violence, sin and disorder. Consequent-
ly, there follows in the psalm a prayer for God to destroy
the wicked. It seems that if God is that close to it, he can
effectively get rid of it. If such a struggle of God with evil
seems strange and mysterious, well the psalmist delights
in mystery. Darkness is not dark to God. And during the
mysterious moments of an infant's being knitted "in my
mother's womb," God was present achieving that wonder.

Throughout the Bible, God is immediately present
with sin and death. The entire book of Job develops that
intuition of faith. Job, thoroughly unclean by reason of a
skin disease (and therefore disqualified from community
worship according to Mosaic Laws—Lev 13), will take
his case immediately before God (Job 13:14; 31:35–37).
God is our redeemer, not by suddenly showing up in the
full flush of victory but by wrestling with evil throughout
the long struggle.

Such a God then will appear, right in the midst of
the two men on their way to Emmaus, at once a part of
their questioning and distress, their disappointment and
disbelief, their decision to quit this once wonderful dream
that Jesus was the Messiah, and even give up. Jesus fitted
right in with the two men, keeping stride with their
movements and feelings. Such has been the invisible God

through the centuries, invisible because of his over-whelming closeness to us. We cannot see the hand placed immediately over our eyes!

Jesus first listened to the two men at length so as to become thoroughly one with them. Only then, he said to them: "Did not the Messiah have to undergo all this so as to enter into his glory?" There is actually a note of impatience, for he first replied: "What little sense you have! How slow you are to believe all that the prophets have announced!" God, however, has long been present with ignorant people and with the slow learning process of his human family. Jesus, therefore, began with Moses and proceeded through the two other major parts of the Hebrew Bible, the prophets and the writings. (The latter is also called "psalms" because it is the first book in that section of the Hebrew Scriptures.)

It all fits together, our glorious moments and our disasters, our achievements and our ignorance. Strangely and mysteriously enough, all this is embraced "by the set purpose and plan of God." So close is our God and Savior, that our redemption did not come about by God's bartering some gold or silver, by dealing with us as though he were a distant financier, not even by handing over the world in exchange for us. We were redeemed "by Christ's blood beyond all price," writes St. Peter in today's second reading. This is "the blood of a spotless, unblemished lamb chosen before the world's foundation and revealed for your sake in these last days." "Blood" here signifies much more than Jesus' death on the cross. The reference to the paschal lamb makes it mean the intimate way by which the love of God flowed through the veins and arteries of Hebrew history, through all the moments of the people's lives, when they suffered and died, even when they acted out of ignorance and sinned.

Jesus is always with us as our redeemer, closer than we are to ourselves.

Prayer:

Lord, you console and counsel us, for you are with us, even through the night. We should never be disturbed. We have in you the way to peace and strength. You never abandon us, even in the nether world. Having gone before us along the way, you show us the path to life.

Third Sunday of Easter—"B" Cycle

Acts 3:13–15, 17–19. God fulfilled "what he announced long ago through the prophets: that his Messiah would suffer." God achieved his design for world salvation even through such awkward means as the ignorance of people and their leaders in delivering Jesus over to death.

1 John 2:1–5. Jesus always intercedes for us: he is "an offering for our sins." We are expected to keep his commandments and so to have "the love of God made perfect" in us.

Luke 24:35–48. Jesus, on Easter night, appears to the Eleven, eats with them, and explains that "the Messiah must suffer and rise from the dead."

The purpose of the Acts of the Apostles is not only to root Church development in the early community at Jerusalem but also to point out designated witnesses of the Spirit in the dramatic evolution from Judaism to Christianity. Acts, therefore, stresses a firm continuity, directed by the Holy Spirit, from the Hebrew Scriptures to Jesus, from Jesus to the group of followers at Jerusalem, and from Jerusalem to the world. Within this continuity such extraordinary and surprising leaps take place, almost to make one think that the chain has been broken.

In today's readings we see that God will maintain this continuity despite our sins and ignorance. Peter admitted in one of his earliest discourses at Jerusalem: "Yet I know, my brothers and sisters, that you acted out of ignorance, just as your leaders did. God has brought to fulfillment by this means what he announced long ago. . . . " In his first epistle, John declares that Jesus is always making intercession for our sins and is himself an offering for them and for the sins of all the world. We are seriously warned to keep the commandments; otherwise we are "a liar." But "if anyone should sin," John consoles such a person that God always grants another chance of conversion if they are sincere in their sorrow.

The continuity between Acts and the Hebrew Scriptures is more firmly established by the many Old Testament phrases which reappear in the speeches, like this one of Peter's to the crowd which "rushed over excitedly" after the cure of a cripple. Peter uses quite a few Old Testament titles for Jesus: "his servant," "the Holy One," "the Just One," "the author of life" (in Greek, a "leader" like Moses). The expression "his servant Jesus" links Jesus with the Suffering Servant passages of the prophecy of Isaiah (Is 42:1–7; 49:1–7; 50:4–9; 52:13–53:12).

Continuity then expects us to live and work within the normal institutions of the Church. Just as Israel and particularly the temple turned out to be the line of stability and of union in the centuries before Jesus, so the Church continues that line into the years after Jesus. Loyalty will be seriously tested by the ignorance and sins of members and leaders. Moments will arise when Israel or the Church may not seem worthy of survival, so despondent may we become at the failures to act or the failures in acting badly. In fact, there is almost an inevitability of such mistakes and offenses. Jesus replied: "the Messiah *must* suffer. . . . In his name, penance for the remission of sins is to be preached to all nations, beginning at Jerusalem." If we men and women are to act, and especially to act vigorously, we must face the prospects of mistakes and misjudgments. Part of the essential Christian message is the humility to confess one's sins and the willingness to be corrected.

If we are faithful, humble and hopeful, suddenly God will surprise us with wonderful developments. This style of fulfilling prophecy was announced long ago in the book of Isaiah:

> Things *of the past* I foretold ahead of time.
> They went forth from my mouth and I
> made sure
> that you heard them.
> Suddenly, by surprise, I took action
> and they came to be (Is 48:3).

The Hebrew word for "suddenly, by surprise" indicates that no amount of study and prayer over the Scriptures can prepare people to know exactly what God will do. God can act without warning. It can happen in the very moment that the prophecy is given or is being pondered:

> From *now* I announce new things to you,
> hidden things of which you knew not.
> *Now,* not long ago, they are brought into
> being (Is 48:6–7).

Jesus' death and resurrection, like the cure of the crippled man, are examples of those sudden, surprising turns in events. They seem like a disruption of orderly plans, like a denial of God's will. Reality is turned around and one must rethink all of life and its relationships.

These startling changes are always difficult to accept and to deal with. Even the cure of the cripple, wonderful as it was, must have forced the man, his family and relations to completely revise their style of living and of thinking toward one another. Other actions cut across the routine of life more severely, even more cruelly—like the execution of Jesus. It is all the more baffling because of the elements of human ignorance and malice. We can usually accept what we have time to consider. And if we are responsible for the cause, we are generally willing to accept the outcome. But we pound on the door of temple or church, if our life is upset by accidental deaths or by the calculated malice of someone else.

For all these reasons we badly need the Church, that strong stable line of continuity. Here we can always return, to wait, to pray, to revive faith, to read the Scriptures, to receive instruction, to meditate and be a source of reconciliation. Here in the Church of Jerusalem the Holy Spirit was manifest. And we can begin to see the role of the Spirit within the sudden actions that disrupt our existence. In the Church, then at Jerusalem, now throughout the world, we meet witnesses of the Spirit.

Prayer:

Lord, whenever we call, you answer us. Whenever we are in distress you are ready to console and help us. We believe that you do wonders for those who call upon you. Let the light of your countenance shine upon us. Put

gladness into our heart. We can lie down and sleep peacefully. You bring security to our dwelling.

Third Sunday of Easter—"C" Cycle

Acts 5:27–32, 40–41. The apostles respond to the High
    Priest and the Sanhedrin: God has raised up Jesus
    whom you put to death. So too does the Holy Spirit
    testify to this. The Sanhedrin, however, before dismiss-
    ing the apostles, had them whipped. The apostles re-
    joiced to have been judged worthy of ill-treatment for
    the sake of the Name.
Rev 5:11–14. In a vision about heaven, John heard the
    voices of many angels, crying out "Worthy is the Lamb
    that was slain to receive power and riches, wisdom and
    strength, honor and glory and praise!"
John 21:1–14 (or 21:1–19). Miraculous haul of fishes. Je-
    sus prepares a meal and eats with his disciples. (Longer
    reading adds the solemn commissioning of Peter and
    the prediction that he will die a martyr.)

These readings present a miniature history of the
Church, and in doing so they alert us to weakness and trials within the Church.

Very clearly we find here a classic example of con-
frontation and dispute within the Church. This time the
struggle is seen with Judaism. We must recall that the
first disciples at Jerusalem still considered themselves
thoroughly Jewish and completely within the legitimate
structure of Judaism. Like the Lord Jesus they faithfully
went up to the temple and followed the Jewish laws about
food and bathing. The High Priest and especially the leg-
islative body called the Sanhedrin did not know what to
make of it. They had handed Jesus over to be executed by

the Romans. Yet at this moment they did not act with the same resolve against Jesus' disciples. They hoped that the whole incident about Jesus would go away. Earlier, in Acts 4, they had dismissed the apostles with no other warning than not to speak in Jesus' name. Peter and John had even replied:

> Judge for yourselves whether it is right in God's sight for us to obey you rather than God. Surely we cannot help speaking of what we have heard and seen (Acts 4:19–20).

Now in Chapter 5 the Sanhedrin are faced with the growing number of disciples and with a fire of enthusiasm spreading among all the people because of signs and wonders (Acts 5:12–16). This time they took more stern action and had the apostles whipped, a humiliating and cruel punishment. (Roman citizens were always exempted from this punishment—Acts 22:25–29.) Yet, indecision still kept the Sanhedrin divided. In a section of Chapter 5, omitted from this Sunday's reading, a member of the Sanhedrin, the Pharisee Gamaliel, exhorted the members of this high court to show some restraint: "Think twice about what you are going to do with these men." He mentioned a number of false messiahs and concluded:

> My advice is that you have nothing to do with these men. Let them alone. If their purpose or activity is human in its origins, it will destroy itself. If, on the other hand, it comes from God, you will not be able to destroy them without fighting God himself (Acts 5:38–39).

Other difficult moments of Church life are presented

to us in these readings. The longer reading of the gospel reminds us again about Peter's three-fold denial of Jesus and the necessity now of pledging his love to Jesus three times. Church leadership evidently must maintain a humble stance; it too remembers its own faults and denials. To bring sinners to the redeemer, leaders must know thoroughly their own need of Jesus from their personal weakness. Peter's denial will show up again in his martyrdom. Jesus states that Peter will be led against his will, like a very elderly person incapable of caring for himself. This moment too is turned by Peter into a beautiful expression of devoted love. Peter asks to be crucified upside down, for he is not worthy to die as his Master did.

Many times we prefer Church leaders without any faults, without the memory of any failures. We will not tolerate their indecision, much less their bad judgment. We fail to show the patient tolerance that we ourselves need and want. We want leadership different from ourselves.

To fail in tolerance means that we cannot give Church leaders the time and space to discuss an issue and to learn. Peter and the apostles were clear and outspoken with the Sanhedrin, but they did not demand an immediate conversion from them. Nor did they require a settlement of how their own apostolic authority harmonized with the legitimate authority of the Jewish leaders. The long book of the Acts of the Apostles shows how much time was necessary to resolve some of these crucial questions.

All the while, Church authority evolved. The role of Peter became more recognized and he appears prominently throughout many New Testament books. Yet, even that position of Peter had rough moments, particularly when confronted by Paul (Gal 2:11–14). Just as the

Sanhedrin had to come gradually to a final decision about Christianity, likewise the Church had no immediate answer about the reception of gentiles into its midst. It was not clear whether or not they should be obligated to keep the entire Jewish law.

Just as leadership and theology developed slowly in the Church, the liturgy of the Christian community took time. At first the disciples worshiped in the temple and broke the bread of their Eucharist privately at home. The book of Revelation reflects a later period of time when the eucharistic liturgy had been expanded into public celebration and was replacing the temple or synagogue services.

We too need to learn the lesson of patience and tolerance. Great ideas need time to work their way, not only through our own individual psyche and emotional life, but also through the larger community of parish, diocese and universal Church. We must always be true to our conscience and rejoice if we are counted worthy to suffer for the name of Jesus. Yet, even then we do not hastily force the issue nor give an ultimatum to others. God wants more than the triumph of truth; he desires truth that sanctifies, that brings greater prayer, justice and forgiveness.

Prayer:

Lord, your anger lasts but a moment; your good will, a lifetime. At nightfall we may weep, but with dawn we will certainly rejoice. You never abandon us. You change our mourning into dancing. We praise you, Lord, for you have rescued us.

Fourth Sunday of Easter—"A"Cycle

Acts 2:14, 36–41. Peter, on Pentecost, preaches that "the whole house of Israel should know ... that God has made both Lord and Messiah this Jesus whom you crucified." The people must reform and be baptized.

1 Pet 2:20–25. Peter continues his baptismal instruction that the newly baptized follow in the suffering footsteps of Jesus, who brought our sins to the cross. By his wounds we are healed.

John 10:1–10. The opening section of John's well known "Good Shepherd" discourse. Jesus is the shepherd whose sheep go in and out for pasture.

As we realize ever more forcefully the intimacy of Jesus within our daily lives, we also understand how exalted and how transcendent he is. The closer we feel his presence, the more his divinity overwhelms us. As we appreciate Jesus' share in our sufferings and even in our death, we sense the power of the resurrection in his godhead.

This unusual development contrasts with what often happens in human friendship. Usually when we come to know someone better, especially when we live closely with them on a daily basis, we begin to notice their idiosyncrasies. We see ever more clearly their faults and deliberate sins.

With Jesus it is dramatically different. As we experience Jesus' immediate presence, his goodness shows up *our* faults, not his. We realize the small extent of our charity. The light of his love causes the barrier of our prejudice and infidelities to cast a heavy shadow. Yet, strangely enough, at this point where human friendship would suffer severe tension and possibly break up, we find Jesus bearing our sins, even united with us in our failures. St. Paul once wrote:

> For our sakes God made him who did not know sin, *to be sin*, so that in him we might become the very holiness of God (2 Cor 5:21).

This development of intimacy with Jesus, his presence even in our sinfulness, yet our gradual awareness of his ever-greater holiness and even his divinity, is what we find in the sequence of today's readings. In the gospel there is the familial closeness of Jesus as our Shepherd. There is only a hint of his divinity.

When the apostles first began their ministry after Pentecost, their first goal was to set the record straight. They concentrated principally on the resurrection of Jesus. From this point they moved back to his Passion and death, in order to explain how the Messiah could have ever come to such an end. For this they searched the Scriptures and delayed principally over the Servant Songs of Isaiah (Is 42:1–7; 49:1–9a; 50:4–9a; 52:13–53:12). When attending to the further instruction of converts, the Church found it necessary to gather together the various statements, parables and disputes of Jesus. In the course of this development, more and more focus was directed to the person of Jesus and eventually to his origin. The divinity of Jesus grew within the awareness of the apostles. We recall Jesus' reply to Philip: "Philip, after I have been with you all this time, you still do not know me" (John 14:9).

Yet, from the very start the apostles realized that Jesus was much more than they could ever appreciate. Spontaneous hints of his divinity began to appear. In Peter's Pentecost address, the apostles remarked that "God had made both Lord and Messiah this Jesus whom you crucified." "Lord" represents the Greek *kurios* and the Hebrew *yahweh*, the proper name for God in the Old Testament. Peter does not delay over this insight. Rather he was more concerned with the question how Jesus' violent death could fit into God's plan for Israel. Jesus, also according to Peter, sent the Holy Spirit, the gift necessary for salvation. Only God bestowed this gift in Old Testament times (*cf.* Joel Ch 3).

The same hints about Jesus' divinity show up in the parable of the Good Shepherd, the first part of which is given in today's liturgy. This sermon draws upon earlier prophetical texts like Jeremiah 23:1–8 and especially Ezechiel 34:1–31. In these Old Testament passages, God is the Good Shepherd. It seems, therefore, that the examples used by Jesus or the later New Testament writers generally reached beyond the goodness and capacity of human beings. Spontaneously or intuitively they hinted of someone superhuman, whom they realized gradually and then firmly to be divine, one of the three persons of the Holy Trinity.

Yet, these developments toward Jesus' divinity took place as the humanity of Jesus was appreciated ever more intimately. The example of the shepherd resonates the closest bonds of human life. Arab children grow up with their pet lamb or sheep, and the two are inseparable. If one of these children has the chore of guarding the family olive tree, the pet lamb or sheep is always at the child's side. Sheep from different shepherds will be mingling together, grazing or drinking at a water hole. In Jesus' parable they are together for the evening in the sheepfold. Each shepherd has only to make distinctive sounds and the sheep immediately separate and follow their master.

Jesus is the shepherd, we the sheep. Or the image can change. (Hebrew literature can delight in clashing images!) Jesus is now the gate leading to the safety of the sheepfold or to the pasture. To pass through this gate is to find security and peace, to find food and water. As this intimacy with Jesus enhances one's appreciation of his overwhelming goodness and concern, we are caught up in the mystery of God's infinite love and eternal desire for our happiness.

If we find any faults in our contact with Jesus—and we usually become aware of these when we become close to any friend or loved ones—these sins are our own. As Peter wrote: "In his own body he brought your sins to the cross, so that all of us, dead to sin, could live in accord with God's will. By his wounds you were healed." Jesus bore our sins because of his intense union with each of us. Such was his obedience to his heavenly Father's intention to redeem us. While our sins caused Jesus' death, Jesus' divine life brought not only him but ourselves to new life. In the mystery of this union between Jesus and ourselves, forgiveness reached its most heroic form. Sin that was destructive to us, became transforming in Jesus, for it called forth a spirit of love and pardon, possessed only by God.

Prayer:

Lord, you are our shepherd. You lead us in verdant pastures and give us repose. Your love surrounds us so totally, that only goodness and kindness follow us all the days of our life. No matter where we wander in the business of our lives, you will bring us back through the gate [yourself] into the house or sheepfold where you dwell.

Fourth Sunday of Easter—"B" Cycle

Acts 4:8–12. Peter defends his cure of the cripple as performed in the name of Jesus, who is the stone rejected which has become the cornerstone, the only name through whom there is salvation.

1 John 3:1–2. "We are God's children now. What we shall later be has not yet come to light."

John 10:11–18. The second section of Jesus' parable of the Good Shepherd. The Good Shepherd lays down his life for his sheep, freely yet under a command of the Father, and he also takes it up again. He calls each sheep by name. There is to be one fold as there is only one shepherd.

This Sunday's readings proclaim confidently that each of us, individually or as a community of believers, contains hidden resources that will eventually transform our whole existence in a wonderful way. This secret quality is often neglected, perhaps ridiculed, at times feared, and in Jesus' case the cause of his death. Yet it is also the cornerstone upon which God will construct the temple of his glory in each of us.

In Acts, Peter must defend the micracle of healing a cripple. Why would anyone be fearful about healing a man unable to walk? In the first epistle of John, the apostle speaks of a hidden source of life which has not yet come to light. And the gospel announces the obvious fact which most of us do not know how to deal with. We will all be one fold, one family, one in love, one in sharing all that we possess. This ecumenical call reaches across churches, nations, races and ethnic groups. If we are fearful of the consequences of such a call, perhaps we can understand a little bit why the people demanded of Peter an account for curing the poor cripple. What would happen to society and its balance or imbalance of wealth, if suddenly all deprived people and underdeveloped nations could run as fast as the rest of us privileged people? We, too, would summon the miracle workers for an explanation.

The disciples were a threat to the Jewish leaders. Caiaphas, the high priest for that year, expressed it succinctly to the ruling class of the Sanhedrin:

> You have no understanding whatever! Can you
> not see that it is better for you to have one man
> die than to have the whole nation destroyed?
> (John 11:50).

To accept Jesus as savior means then that we must be open to the beauty and potential of life all around us. What we despise may be the source of our salvation. What we try to suppress in ourselves may be able to turn our lives around enthusiastically toward God. The gentleness which gets in the way of our hard business deals, the generosity which will restrict the luxuries in our own homes, the confidence in others which leaves us open to being taken advantage of at times—all of these beautiful virtues tend to be suppressed—like Jesus on the cross. This is why Jesus is "the stone rejected ... which becomes the cornerstone." Jesus summons these hidden qualities back to life. Jesus calls us to see great possibilities in others. Like Peter we are asked to cure the cripples in our midst. By accepting people despite our prejudice and fears and by assuring them of their great potential for good, we enable what has been neglected by the "builders" of society to become the cornerstone of a new, happy existence.

These people on the fringe of society are the ones to

whom Jesus naturally turned, the unwashed shepherds, the filthy foreigners, the traitorous tax-collectors, the abused prostitutes, the lepers supposedly non-existent and unseen by the rest of men and women. They have become the cornerstone. Because of his attention to them, Jesus was neglected and hounded to death. Jesus becomes the cornerstone by his association with the poor and oppressed. He thus shows up as the savior of all oppressed people, ourselves in our sins.

To these people Jesus bestowed the love that belongs only within the family. He says to them, in the words of John's first letter:

> Dearly beloved,
> you are God's children now;
> what you shall later be has not yet come to
>   light.
> ... when it comes to light,
> you shall be like him.

The poor shall be like Jesus because he became so much like them! We cannot know Jesus independently of his family, the poor and the neglected.

Jesus snatched them from the grasp of the wolf. He put himself in their place and so laid down his life for his sheep. In doing so, Jesus gave an extraordinary dignity to these outlaws and non-people. They became his very own, called by name. And as they rose to new life, they imparted this life of theirs to Jesus. These statements may seem to reverse the entire story of salvation. Yet, for some reason or another, if the poor did not turn to Jesus, his death would have no meaning. After all, he laid down his life for them.

Jesus, moreover, died for *all* men and women.

> I have other sheep
> that do not belong to this fold.
> I must lead them, too,
> and they shall hear my voice.
> There shall be one flock, one shepherd.

No one is wealthy, if separate from Jesus. Only in the Lord can the hidden possibilities of any person be brought to light and granted the strength to develop. Jesus calls all of us then to cure the cripple in the rest of us. We are all that cripple. We all must hear the voice of Jesus and be healed in his name. This is the command which Jesus received from his Father. Yet it so thoroughly resonates in him, that

> I lay down my life. . . .
> No one takes it from me;
> I lay it down *freely.*

When we can respond that quickly—that freely—to the hidden goodness in others, then we are acting of our own accord and at the same time following the most serious command from the Father.

Prayer:
Blessed is that one who comes in the name of the Lord and speaks that hidden name by which a secret part of ourselves comes alive after years of neglect. Blessed is that hopeful person who sees such goodness in us as to enable us to run and dance where we once were cripples. Blessed is that person who brings to light what we shall be as God's children.

Fourth Sunday of Easter—"C" Cycle

Acts 13:14, 43–52. Many converts and persecution at Pisidian Antioch. Many Jewish people joined in accepting Jesus as the Messiah, others resisted, even vigorously. The apostles Paul and Barnabas turn all the
   more firmly to the gentiles.

Rev 7:9, 14–17. In vision John sees a huge crowd from
   every nation and race, gathering before the throne of
   the lamb. "The lamb will shepherd them" and these
   will never again hunger or thirst.

John 10:27–30. My sheep know me, says Jesus, and no
   one can snatch them out of my hand.

A monumental decision was made at the city of Pisidian Antioch. Paul and Barnabas were in the midst of
their first missionary journey. They with the apostle
Mark had set out from another city also by the name of
Antioch, now in Syria near its border with Turkey, and
from there sailed to Cyprus. Because of many severe difficulties, first at sea and then through the rugged mountains around Pisidian Antioch and finally from hostile or
jealous people, Mark deserted Paul and Barnabas. Paul
never forgot this moment of weakness. Later at the start
of the second missionary journey a sharp disagreement
arose between Paul and Barnabas whether or not to take
Mark along. As a result, the two separated, and Barnabas
took Mark with him and sailed for Cyprus! (Acts
15:36–39).

But other problems arose at Pisidian Antioch. This
time it was the problem of success! We are told that
"many Jews and devout Jewish converts [the latter would
be gentiles who attached themselves to the synagogue but
without circumcision and full observance] became their
followers." We read further that "on the following sab-

bath, almost the entire city gathered to hear the word of God." This overcrowding by gentiles antagonized some of the Jewish people, not all, for quite a few Jews aligned themselves with Paul and Barnabas and accepted Jesus as the Messiah. Ever more jealous of Paul's success, they "countered with violent abuse whatever Paul said." Jealousy among religiously minded people has always been, and still is one of the most difficult phenomena to deal with!

At this point Paul makes one of the most important announcements of the entire Bible:

> The word of God has to be declared to you
> [who are Jewish] first of all; but since you reject
> it, *we now turn to the gentiles.*

The Hebrew Scriptures had been struggling with this idea of universal salvation for centuries. There have been hints of such a decision strewn throughout the Bible, texts like that of Isaiah and Micah in which many nations shall stream toward the mountain of the Lord's house (Is 2:2–4; Mic 4:1–3) or others of Jeremiah that "all nations will be gathered together to honor the name of the Lord at Jerusalem" (Jer 3:17). Yet, these passages never moved to the center of the prophets' thinking nor became carefully integrated as a major part of their theology. The passages were more like unusual insights, too beautiful to abandon, too demanding to implement. The right moment had not yet come (*cf.* Eccles 3:1–8).

But now with Paul and Barnabas at Pisidian Antioch "the appointed time" arrived. As we have seen, it was a time of severe tension for Paul and Barnabas. They must have been physically tired, maybe near exhaustion. Emotionally they were caught up in the excitement of many new converts and the enthusiastic reception by all the city. Then when they were on such a high, sustained only by the contagious inspiration of the moment, a notable group of people reacted jealously and angrily.

Paul replies calmly, clearly, courageously. He did not back down. With fearless determination he spoke the words that would ring throughout the world: "We now turn to the gentiles!" Paul did not realize all the consequences. He was too intelligent not to be aware of the theological difficulties to be raised by the Jewish Christians who practiced the Mosaic law and its customs. Not even the famous Council of Jerusalem, recorded in Acts 15, was able to settle the issue. Paul himself would struggle through two major epistles, Galatians and Romans, to clarify the case for himself and for the Church.

Great inspirations are always that way. While we are moved to accept—maybe forced by our conscience—we cannot measure all the results. Our principal support lies in an attitude to live and pray within the Church, normally to check out our ideas with others, always to be willing to abide by further decisions. All through this process, whether it be prayer, discussion or the Jerusalem Council, Paul continually interacted with great prudence and brilliant dialogue. He took full responsibility for his great inspirations.

The decision to "turn to the gentiles" did not mean that non-Jewish people were all under God's condemnation up to this moment. Even without knowing Yahweh, the God of Israel, or Jesus, his Son incarnate, they still had a chance of eternal life. We can apply to them the words of Jesus in the gospel:

My sheep hear my voice . . .
[though it be indistinctly without knowing

the speaker]
I give them eternal life,
and they shall never perish ...
There is no snatching out of his [the Father's]
    hand.

Neither was there any conscious way of being united in God. As a result, many aberrations and strange ways of thinking and acting showed up among the gentiles.

Only through Israel was union to be achieved. Only because of God's chosen people would knowledge of the true God and Lord of the universe be made known. This new tremendous relationship would be accomplished in an unusual way—not by military force, nor by intellectual arguments, but by a firm sense of dedication to the Lord Jesus, by visible sincerity, by a grasp of the Scriptures, by fidelity to one's conscience, by a humble attitude toward others.

Some of these virtues show up in John's vision of heaven. A sense of humble kindliness and serene peace shows up in the statement: "Never again shall they know hunger or thirst. . . . The Lamb will lead them to springs of life-giving water, and God will wipe every tear from their eyes." We find also a strange reversal in the phrase: "the Lamb on the throne will shepherd them." Usually the shepherd leads the lamb and sheep. A lowly person, willingly offered in sacrifice as the lamb of God, brings salvation. Those who follow the lamb have passed through a "great period of trial." The redemption of all nations will not happen easily, but happen it must and it will.

Prayer:

Lord, we are the people whom you shepherd. Enable us always to respond vigorously to your inspiration, whatever be the cost of personal comfort and ambition. May we be your instruments like Paul, opening your flock to many others.

Fifth Sunday of Easter—"A" Cycle

Acts 6:1–7. A quarrel developed between Greek-speaking disciples and those who spoke Hebrew and was solved by ordaining the first deacons to care for widows and the needy among the former. Many Jewish priests embraced the faith.

1 Pet 2:4–9. In this continuation of an early baptismal liturgy, Peter compares Christians to "living stones . . . a holy priesthood" and to "a stone . . . rejected."

John 14:1–12. Jesus prepares many dwelling places in his Father's house. He is the way, the truth and the life. Whoever sees Jesus, sees the Father.

In the scriptural selections for this Sunday the priesthood of all baptized Christians is given special attention. This theme comes foward in many different ways, for instance: the conversion of many Jewish priests and the institution of the order of deacons indicate that a new style of leadership is emerging in the early Church. Up till now in Judaism, a priest was that person of the male sex born not only of the tribe of Levi but also of the family of Aaron within that tribe. This regulation became very clear in the postexilic age. Not only did the apostles not come exclusively, if at all, from the Levitical tribe, but they shared some of their own religious duties with seven men chosen not for their ancestral background but for being "deeply spiritual and prudent." Priesthood then was being quietly extended.

A more democratic style of government is also evident. The Twelve said to the entire assembly of Christians, "Look around among your own number." The community selected the seven new deacons and presented them to the apostles "who first prayed over them and then imposed hands on them." The congregation was sharing in the selection process and attended carefully to the holiness and prudence of the candidates.

Theologically too the special privileges of Israel were being granted gentiles. Words once directed to the people Israel, that "you are 'a chosen race, a royal priesthood, a consecrated nation, a people he claims for his own to proclaim the glorious works' of the One who called you," now consecrate all people as God's special possession. We should note in passing that the privilege of being "a royal priesthood" never denied the existence in Israel of a special order of priests, called the Levites, neither does this title of "royal priesthood" prevent the Church from possessing a distinct order of "ordained priests." At the same time this baptismal instruction in the first letter of Peter insists that all Christians share in the priestly responsibility of prayer and instruction, of forgiveness and reconciliation.

It is this common priesthood that strikes us as important in today's readings. The gospel implies little or no importance upon the presence of ordained mediators. Thomas had asked Jesus to know the way that Jesus takes to the Father. Jesus replied to him and to all his disciples:

I am the way, and the truth, and the life;
no one comes to the Father but through me.

In knowing Jesus we are already on the *way*; in following Jesus we are assured of the *truth*; in consecration to Jesus we share his *life*.

Such a statement does not deny the role of theology

in struggling to express the truth accurately, just as earlier in First Peter a special order of ordained priests was not being negated. Yet, a solitary warning is given to all of us, and especially to those among us who tend to become involved in serious theological disputes. It is possible to argue so fiercely about the theology of the Eucharist or of resurrection, that our anger and disrespect have denied the charity which is the supreme gift of God, greater even than faith and hope (1 Cor 13:13). Moreover, we have forgotten the special presence of Jesus, who is "the truth."

Whether in theological school or in family instruction, nothing is gained and the best is lost, if arguments violate charity and make the presence of Jesus highly uncomfortable, perhaps impossible.

As we contemplate Jesus, by reading the Scriptures, by participating in Church liturgy, by realizing his presence in friends and strangers (for whom there are "many dwelling places in my Father's house"), we also have a vision of God the Father. We come to sense the wondrous mystery of the Holy Trinity: the Father, Jesus, and the bond between them of the Holy Spirit. At this point all theological statements drop from our mind. No sentences can measure up to such a wonder of love and to such an exchange of all that each possesses and by which the best in each becomes the person of the other. Contemplation such as this wraps us in silence.

It may seem strange that a series of biblical passages which began with a quarrel between Greek and Hebrew speaking Christians over the distribution of alms has led us to a contemplation of the Holy Trinity. At the center of this transition, however, has been the expectation of charity. Each moment of generous love can be the door to ecstatic love in God.

Prayer:

Lord, the earth is full of your kindness. We want to respond with respect to everyone. We sense a holy fear that might hurt or injure this love so delicate and fragile around about us. Give us your patience and your prudence, so that we can follow you, our way, through this path of goodness which leads us to our heavenly home.

Fifth Sunday of Easter—"B" Cycle

Acts 9:26–31. Upon Paul's first visit to Jerusalem the disciples there are still afraid of him. He must be whisked away when an attempt is made on his life by Greek-speaking Jews. Meanwhile, the Church throughout all Judea, Galilee and Samaria was at peace.

1 Jn 3:18–24. Let us love in deed and in truth and not just talk about it. God's commandment is this: to believe in the name of his Son, Jesus Christ, and to love one another.

John 15:1–8. Jesus is the true vine, we are the branches, the Father is the vinegrower.

Today we meditate upon the intimate bond between ourselves within the Church. In Acts, Paul is determined to maintain close unity and makes the first of six visits to the mother church at Jerusalem. This unity is to be practical, "not just talk," as we are seriously reminded in the first epistle of John. In the gospel we are attached to one another like branches which grow from a single stock of vine.

When Paul, the ex-persecutor and rabid zealot of the pharisee sect, first returned to Jerusalem as a disciple of Jesus, "they were all afraid of him." The members of the mother church "even refused to believe that he was a disciple." We are then told that faithful Barnabas, clear in his judgments, always kind and forgiving, prudent and trusted by the others, "took him in charge and introduced him to the apostles. He explained to them how on his journey Saul had seen the Lord." Later when Paul (as Saul came to be called) secluded himself first in the desert and then at his hometown of Tarsus, Barnabas "brought him back to Antioch" to launch Paul on his extraordinary ministry (Acts 11:25-26) and still later, unfortunately, when Barnabas defended Mark's right for another chance (Acts 15:36-39; see also Fourth Sunday of Easter, "C" Cycle), Paul adamantly refused. We begin to understand not only the different temperaments of the first disciples but also the fear of that firebrand and determined apostle, Paul. Unity was not a simple, easy matter for the early Church, yet it remained one body with many members, and the body was Christ (1 Cor 12).

Six times Paul returned to Jerusalem. Though he was equal to the other twelve apostles and seemed always in the thick of some controversy with them—particularly over the necessity of gentile converts to be circumcised and to obey the dietary laws—still, Paul never had the least thought of founding his own church. Not only did Paul manifest this strong attachment to the one Church, but this Church in its turn adopted Paul's epistles as a part of its Bible. Paul's epistles with the gospels constitute the major source for Church doctrine and morals today.

In the gospel reading, John develops the intimacy and the cost of Church unity. Jesus says:

I am the vine, you are the branches.
The one who lives in me and I in that one,
will produce abundantly,
for apart from me you can do nothing.

From this comparison it were as though all of us shared the same blood which flowed through a common network of arteries and veins. Jesus is the heart whose rhythmic beat sends the blood coursing through us. The life and strength of one person are the vitality and sustenance of the other. Even the secret thoughts of one member will have an effect, good or bad, upon the others. No member can be totally healthy if any other member is sickly. Anyone who separates himself from the vine "is like a withered, rejected branch, picked up to be thrown in the fire and burnt."

Every vine must be pruned, so as "to increase the yield." No branch, then, can selfishly seek its own good, independent of others. Usually such a branch turns out to be a parasite or "sucker" which must be effectively trimmed away. Pruning can be painful, for in the life of the Church it means cutting back on activities which the entire "vine" cannot sustain. The new growth may be healthy yet preventing fruit from forming on the vine.

Pruning is not enough for a healthy vine. A vine must be fertilized, watered and nurtured. Jesus speaks of "my words [which] stay part of you." We, the branches, need to be nourished by the "word" which comes to us from the "vine," the Church. For this reason we celebrate the liturgy, and the fruit of the vine is transformed into the eucharistic cup. Other forms of nourishment and strength for the branches consist in prayer and in peaceful surrender to what is known to be the will of Jesus.

The first epistle of John adds further advice to sustain a strong unity within the Church. Most of all, "let us love in deed and in truth and not just talk about it." John goes so far as to say that "love" is "our way of knowing that we are committed to the truth and are at peace before God." Then comes the startling statement: "no matter what our consciences may charge us with." John is aware that we can often be disturbed by false consciences, scrupulous consciences. A false conscience thinks that it does all that God wants if it keeps the letter of the law— and yet may be selfishly offending charity! A scrupulous conscience inflicts its problems and fears upon everyone else and so restricts charity. We must rest our case primarily with God who commands us to love one another and not with the strange charges of our conscience. "God is greater than our hearts and all is known to him."

Without charity, a unified church is not worthy of survival. Without church unity, charity cannot exist, as people are too separated, one from the other, to fully love one another.

We need to question ourselves, lest we drift away doctrinally or morally, theoretically, emotionally or practically, from the main body of our Church and especially from our religious leaders. Do we make a generous, forgiving love the first principle of our conscience? Do we place the strength and fruitfulness of the entire vine before our own individual pleasure or advantage?

Prayer:

I praise you, Lord, in the assembly of the Church. Here the lowly and the hungry gather to participate in generous charity. Give me the confidence to bring my needs to the Church; give me the generosity to respond to the prayers and sorrows of my neighbor. Let me always realize that as branches on the one vine, none of us can be happy if one of us is still suffering.

Fifth Sunday of Easter—"C" Cycle

Acts 14:21–27. Paul and Barnabas complete the first missionary journey and report to the community at Antioch which had commissioned them. They relate all that God had helped them accomplish and repeat the need to undergo many trials perseveringly.

Rev 21:1–5. John sees a vision of the new heavens and the new earth, also the new Jerusalem, beautiful as a bride. Every tear will be wiped away.

John 13:31–33, 34–35. Jesus will soon depart and recommends love for each other, "such as my love has been for you."

This Sunday is the day of remembrance and gratitude. We thank God for Paul and Barnabas' apostolic accomplishments, Jesus' legacy of charity, John's vision of heavenly glory. We need to recall and to celebrate great achievements that happen in our midst. In fact our faith and our perseverance depend upon this response of ours. Jesus summed it up very well when he declared that the Eucharist is performed "in remembrance."

Biblically, remembrance is much more than recalling the past. Like the Eucharist it is most of all a celebration in the present moment. Again, however, this festivity is much more than making merry over a great event of long ago. Remembrance is re-living now what was done then. For that reason when liturgical celebrations come to the heart of the action, the narrative style is abandoned and the celebrant speaks in the first person of God himself:

Take this, all of you, and eat it:
this is *my* body which will be given up for
you . . .

this is the cup of *my* blood,
the blood of the *new* and everlasting covenant.

The contemporaneity of the remembered event is
emphasized throughout the book of Deuteronomy, a liturgical book for the most part of sermons and other
sanctuary activities. Although written several centuries
after Moses, still it writes:

Hear, O Israel, the statutes and decrees which I
proclaim in your hearing *this day* . . . The Lord,
our God, made a covenant *with us* at Horeb
[i.e., Sinai]; not with our ancestors . . . but *with
us, all of us who are alive here this day.* The
Lord spoke *with you face to face* on the mountain from the midst of the fire (Deut 5:1–4).

Therefore, when Paul and Barnabas returned from
the first missionary journey, "they called the congregation together and related all that God had helped them
accomplish, and how he opened the door of faith to the
gentiles." The entire group of disciples at Antioch partic-
ipated in the joy and wonder of the extraordinary spread
of the faith.

Earlier, when they had commissioned the two apostles, Paul and Barnabas, the inspiration had come in the
middle of the eucharistic liturgy. They had all been fasting, as the text points out, and the Holy Spirit spoke
through a prophet in their midst: "Set apart Barnabas
and Paul for me. . . . " Then after further fasting and
prayer, they imposed hands on them and sent them forth.
To impose hands is to set up a unity of spirit and responsibility; it is to form one "person" or one "Church."

The reference to fasting in the ceremony of commissioning can be tied with Paul's mention of suffering in his missionary journey. He put it this way: "We must undergo many trials if we are to enter into the reign of God." Fasting is a real, though symbolic way of accompanying the missionary in his laborious travels. It is remembrance in the flesh and a participation in the spirit of what is happening in other parts of the Church. Remembrance is living now those wonderful, though difficult moments of Church life.

When the cycle of readings includes a passage from the book of Revelation, remembrance also reaches into the distant future. We re-live the wonderful moment to come at the end of time. "The former heavens and the former earth had passed away." John "saw new heavens and a new earth." The Church is now absorbed into the new Jerusalem, "the holy city, coming down out of heaven from God, beautiful as a bride prepared to meet her husband." Because Jesus is already in the midst of this final glory and Jesus is also present with us in the liturgy, our remembrance can introduce such moments into our liturgy.

The happiness at Antioch over remembering Paul and Barnabas' missionary triumphs can be linked with the eternal joy of Jesus and the saints in heaven. This connection is made for us by the gospel, introduced by the statement of Jesus:

Now is the Son of Man glorified
and God is glorified in him. . .
My children, I am not to be with you much
        longer.

Jesus will leave his disciples by the painful way of the cross. Again we recall Paul's words: "We must undergo many trials if we are to enter into the reign of God." Jesus, on his part, makes that suffering all the more possible to endure. He adds the "new commandment: Love one another. Such as my love has been for you, so must your love be for each other."

Remembrance combines past, present and future, suffering and glory, hopes and fulfillment. The liturgy of the Eucharist enables us to do much more than we ever anticipated, for it brings the *mirabilia Dei,* the wondrous deeds of God, from the past right into our contemporary actions. Moreover, the liturgy never allows us to forget the certainty of the new Jerusalem.

Prayer:

Lord, I will praise your name for ever. In the moment of prayer all your works sing out your praise. Never let us forget your gracious and merciful love. This goodness extends not only from creation to the new heavens and new earth, but it surrounds my entire existence. Your kingdom is a kingdom for all ages, and your dominion endures through all generations.

Sixth Sunday of Easter—"A" Cycle

Acts 8:5–8, 14–17. Philip the deacon evangelizes Samaria. Peter and John come to impose hands that the newly baptized persons may receive the Holy Spirit.

1 Pet 3:15–18. "Speak gently and respectfully" when asked about "this hope of yours." It is better to suffer for good deeds than for evil ones. "This is why Christ died for sins once for everyone."

John 14:15–21. Jesus promises the Spirit of truth. Therefore you will not be orphaned. "I am in the Father, and you in me, and I in you."

Even though Easter celebrates the resurrection and departure of Jesus from our earthly existence, the liturgical readings emphasize that "I, Jesus, will not leave you orphaned." We are intimately aware of Jesus' presence. This Easter season which draws many of its biblical passages from the Acts of the Apostles and the gospel of John keeps our thoughts within the context of Church unity (no matter how far the Church spreads) and within liturgical or sacramental celebration. To be at peace we need the secure and loving home of the Church.

The episode of Philip the deacon in Samaria brings out very effectively the ties which must exist between the churches and the Mother Church at Jerusalem, between later ordained ministers like Philip and the first apostles, Peter and John.

Wonderful things happened in Samaria through the ministry of Philip. He preached eloquently that Jesus was the Messiah. He performed miracles. Crowds "attended closely to what he had to say." Finally, the narrator remarks: "The rejoicing in that town rose to fever pitch." It would seem that little else was necessary; the church of Samaria was launched on its way.

The Mother Church of Jerusalem felt it necessary to send Peter and John. These apostles prayed, imposed hands and were thus God's instruments for imparting the Holy Spirit. Luke, the author of Acts, carefully distinguishes here between the sacrament of baptism and that of confirmation, between the action of the deacon and that of the apostle.

Church structure is not meant to stifle. If the Holy Spirit comes through the ministry of the church, then there is excitement, exuberance, enthusiasm. This gift of joy, one of the special gifts of the Spirit (Gal 5:22; Rom 14:17), is most genuine when it exudes gentleness and peace. This is exactly the exhortation in the second reading. Writing to the newly baptized—the kind of persons to whom Peter and John ministered in Samaria—Peter urges them to "speak gently and respectfully."

Gentleness is nurtured within the security of a good home and a loving family. Because each member is concerned about the other, it is not necessary to argue, shout or threaten. The bonds between the family-members impart an intuitive insight into the needs of the other. The trust between persons grants the privilege to think, to be silent, to have time and space. This family spirit ought to prevail within the Church. Peter put it this way:

> Venerate the Lord ... in your hearts. Should anyone ask you the reason for this hope of yours be ever ready to reply, but speak gently and respectfully. Keep your conscience clear.

There is strength about this gentleness. Each one has a reason for his actions and "this hope of yours," and is ready to offer it. "But gently!" The bond of friendship and love, evidently, is more important than triumph in a shouting match or even more important than clever debating that squelches and humiliates the other person.

No family is perfect, no set of ideals is maintained with absolute purity. At this time another type of gentleness is necessary. Here we *wait* with hope for the other person to realize his mistake. We do not rub it in nor glory in his collapse. Just as Jesus, a "just man [died] for the sake of the unjust, so that he could lead you to God," we ought to imitate Jesus when a member of our family fails.

The gospel of John offers a few more suggestions for the strength of our family bond within the Church. Twice, at the beginning and toward the end, the gospel speaks of love with *obedience.* "The one who obeys the commandments from me is the person who loves me." Every home relies upon discipline—the self-control to respect others in their privacy, the strength to remain silent lest another in the family be embarrassed, the ability to keep secrets, the prudence to know when to overlook a fault and when to offer advice and even a warning.

This type of self-control relies upon the Spirit of Truth whom Jesus promises to send to those who love him and keep his commandments. This Spirit is such that "the world cannot accept" its inspiration. Here is another source of discipline, necessary for healthy growth within a family. No one ought to be swayed by forces outside the family—whether this be peer pressure, or advertisements, or normal temptations that invade the sexuality or ambitions of every person. With the "Spirit of Truth" a well disciplined person can stand against the tidal wave of the world.

Finally, a happy home and a fervent Church are composed of people with hope. It is interesting to note that the first letter of Peter speaks of giving "the reason for this *hope* of yours." We would have expected to read "faith" instead of "hope." Hopes look to the future and therefore see the mysteries of faith not just as statements in a book but as indicators of how God receives us in the future. Hope carries a sense of vision. Jesus, at the end of today's gospel, also speaks of hopes and visions.

> I too will love that one
> [who obeys my commandments]
> and *reveal myself* to him.

We recall Jesus' other words: "I am the way, the truth, and the life" (John 14:6, see Fifth Sunday of Easter, "A" Cycle). The way and the truth are to be found in the person of Jesus, and then the life which we hope to enjoy for all eternity will be ours already.

The biblical passages for today not only assure us that "I will not leave you orphaned" but they offer practical suggestions how the Church becomes a family of love and hope, centered in Jesus who is both mother and father.

Prayer:

Lord, we sing the words of the psalmist for all the world to hear: Hear now, all you who fear God, while I declare what he has done for me. You have gathered us into one family. Enable us to contribute the hope and discipline, the loyalty and patience, and most of all the love that preserves a family spirit within your Church.

Sixth Sunday of Easter—"B" Cycle

Acts 10:25–26, 34–35, 44–48. When the gentile household of Cornelius received the Spirit and the gift of
tongues, just as the apostles had on the day of Pentecost, Peter ordered them to be baptized at once.

1 John 4:7–10. Not that we have loved God but that he
loved us first.

John 15:9–17. My commandment: love one another as I
have loved you and have laid down my life for you ...
not that you chose me, rather I have chosen you. Go
forth and bear fruit.

We are swept along by God's initiative. The Holy
Spirit suddenly comes upon us, unannounced, even
against Church practice! Before Peter had time to consider the question of baptizing uncircumcised foreigners—
up till then against the practice of the Jerusalem Mother
Church—the Spirit had already descended upon the
household of Cornelius. Here is an example of God's ef-
fective love which silences every objection before it is
spoken, thus "God has first loved us" and given us the
example and even the commandment: thus you are to
love one another.

God has acted before we have time to think about it.
Our reasoning does not create God's goodness, nor measure it—as the prophecy of Isaiah reminds us:

> Who [among you] has cupped in his hand the
> waters of the sea.
> and marked off the heavens with a
> span?
> Who has held in a measure the dust of the
> earth,
> weighed the mountains in scales

> and the hills in a balance?
> Who has directed the spirit of the Lord,
>   or has instructed him as his counselor?
>   (Is 40:12–13)

The wonder of the world is already there before we ever look up to see it—just as there are myriads of stars waiting billions of years to reveal God's wonderful power and goodness for the first visitor to come their way.

Still greater power and goodness are hidden, waiting for us to recognize their existence in ourselves and in our neighbors. God is already accomplishing so very much that his goodness would overwhelm us like an atom bomb were we to see all of it at once. In this context we can understand the oft-repeated statement in the Bible that no one can see God and live: as in the case of Moses (Ex 33:20), the parents of Samson (Judg 13:22), and the prophet Isaiah (Is 6:5). As a matter of fact, all of these persons did "see" God in some mystical, symbolic way, but not face to face, and as a result their entire life was transformed and took a decidedly new direction.

We too would be very surprised if we learned how often we have approached, in some mystical, symbolic way, yet nonetheless truly and really, the wondrous presence of God.

Such was the case with Peter. Messengers from the Roman centurion Cornelius brought Peter to their master's house. Peter was struck at once with their exceptional sincerity and deep goodness. Spontaneously he said: "God has made it clear to me that no one should call anyone unclean or impure . . . God shows no partiality." That statement broke centuries of customs and even of theology, that Israel alone was God's chosen people, separated from all other nations as God's very own (*cf.* Deut 7:6–8; Ex 19:5–6).

Peter was in for still greater surprises. Even before he could consider all the theological implications of baptizing uncircumcised foreigners—recall how long it would take Paul to get this idea fully accepted—the Holy Spirit suddenly and wondrously fell upon the entire household of Cornelius and they prophesied in tongues. At once Peter ordered that they could be baptized without any further delay. On a still later occasion Peter was to falter and delay; he seemed unwilling or afraid to take the full consequences of his action and accept the baptized foreigners as equal in all ways to Jewish Christians (Gal 2:11–14). Evidently it is not easy to accept the presence of the Spirit in foreigners or in people of other religions and races.

Just as Peter had no choice but to baptize the household of Cornelius, we too have no option but to accept what already exists: God's wonderful love in our midst. The first letter of John insists upon this fact. Each line echoes the sublime revelation: God's love is there before we think about it. Because nothing is as contagious or as compelling as love, we are not free to ignore it. We must allow ourselves to be swept along by it and to love supernaturally in return. Such love may summon us, as it did Jesus, to lay down our lives for our friends. Jesus calls this action the obedience with which "I have kept my Father's commandments and so have lived in his love."

Love is an act of the will which somehow or other can take away a person's freedom. Love, it is true, can be a matter of choice, if it depends upon the intellect to weigh the evidence and find the object worthy of love. In the case of Jesus' love and the gift of the Spirit, the evidence so overwhelms the intellect that it cannot measure and weigh the worth and goodness, no more than human instruments can "measure the dust of the earth and weigh the mountains in scales" (see the earlier quotation from Is 40).

We are confronted then with an intuition, a supernatural "feeling," a delicate pledge of the Spirit, a sublime touch of love, a wondrous presence of God. It can be compared to the fire within the burning bush, which did not destroy the bush as fires ought to do, but suddenly turned into the voice of the Lord God, speaking the name of "Moses—Moses!" (Ex 3:4). Although like Moses we may argue and remonstrate, yet somehow or other we realize that to say "No!" would destroy us forever and leave eternal pangs of regret. Such demands of the spirit, such expectations of love, effectively remove our freedom.

These intuitions are the pledges of eternal life, the beginning of our vision of God.

Prayer:

Lord, in secret ways you reveal your saving power and deep within my heart you make a remembrance of your kindness and faithfulness. Enable me to respond immediately. Allow such inspirations to guide my actions, even if it means laying down my life for you or for my neighbor. Then all the ends of the earth will see the salvation by our God.

Sixth Sunday of Easter—"C" Cycle

Acts 15:1–2, 22–29. Some unauthorized members of the Jerusalem church tried to insist upon circumcision as necessary for salvation within the church at Antioch. The Jerusalem Council was called; it decided against the need of following the Mosaic laws, except for a few customary practices involving "blood."

Rev 21:10–14, 22–23. The heavenly Jerusalem fulfills all the hopes of Israel. Symbolically its 12 gates represented the 12 tribes; the 12 courses of stones in the foundation of the wall bore names of the 12 apostles. The Lord God and the lamb took the place of the temple.

John 14:23–29. Rejoice, Jesus says, for he goes away! Then he will send the Holy Spirit to instruct you in everything. Peace is my farewell gift to you.

Easter season stands between the long preparation for the death and resurrection of Jesus and the post-Pentecostal period with its attention upon the spread of the Church. While the Lenten period draws heavily from the Old Testament and so represents the centuries of preparation within Judaism, the weeks of the Church year after Pentecost center not just on Jesus but upon Jesus as the source of Church doctrine and practice. The weeks after Easter act as a bridge between Israel of the Mosaic covenant and the Church of the new covenant. We are faced again with the serious question of continuity.

Continuity there must be! We would have little or no interest in the future, particularly in heaven, if the person in the future would have no relation to the person we are right now! That would actually mean annihilation and the creation of someone else in our place.

We also form one "person" in Jesus, as we are all members of the one body. (See the Fifth Sunday of Easter—"B" Cycle.) This body of the Lord embraces all of our ancestors, reaching back and beyond the patriarchs of the book of Genesis, all of our neighbors across the world today, and all of our descendants. This body of the Lord too must possess continuity, establishing a firm line from Israel of the Hebrew Scriptures to the Church of the new covenant.

We also expect that Jesus who speaks the words of the gospel today within the Church is the same Jesus who first spoke those words during his public ministry or during the forty days after his resurrection from the dead. The Jesus who instructs by word and example and the Church which interprets this message for later ages must be in harmony. Their voices ought to blend. We do not ask or want repetition for the sake of historical accuracy. The Church is not expected to be a graduate school of historical research! The pastoral goals of Jesus must continue with the Church of each succeeding generation. We see, then, that continuity in some way involves evolution and modification. Evolution sometimes means dramatic leaps without breaking the line of loyalty and tradition.

The classical problem of early Christianity revolved around the necessity of the Mosaic law for salvation. Jesus kept it perfectly, from his birth, for he was circumcised on the eighth day (Luke 2:21) and he never annulled the force of the Mosaic law. "Do not think that I have come to abolish the law and the prophets. I have come, not to abolish them, but to fulfill them" (Matt 5:17). Yet, Peter on the impulse of the Spirit had baptized the household of the Roman centurion Cornelius without requiring circumcision (see Sixth Sunday of Easter, "C" Cycle). Paul, too, found this same spontaneous manifestation of the faith among the gentiles (see Fourth Sunday of Easter, "C" Cycle) and so made the exciting declaration: "We now turn to the gentiles!" The controversy over the law was to linger for a long time, so that Paul dedicated to this topic his most comprehensive piece of theological writing, the epistle to the Romans.

An important, doctrinal step along the way was the Council of Jerusalem. The apostles and elders gathered for deliberation and came to an agreement with the whole Mother Church at Jerusalem that the Mosaic laws were not to be required, nor the many traditions of the rabbis, only four customs centering on "blood." The converts, out of courtesy, were asked not to partake of blood, nor of animals improperly slaughtered without draining the blood, nor of strangled animals for the same reason, nor of marriages within certain blood bonds. Therefore, the Council settled a doctrinal issue about circumcision and the Mosaic law, but did it in a way to preserve peace. Certain customs can reach so deeply into people's lives as to cause great unrest if they are brushed aside.

We are thus given a good model for handling questions of continuity today. We ought to take into consideration both the theological issue and the feelings of people. *First*, we must have an attitude of great and awesome respect for every manifestation of the Holy Spirit, as did Peter and Paul in their ministry. Even if the Spirit seemed to shatter the sacred tradition, we have to be calm, respectful and waiting. We might even have to act immediately, like Peter who asked: "What can stop these people who have received the Holy Spirit, even as we have, from being baptized with water?" (Acts 10:47).

Second, before an individual act, much less an intuition or a second sense, can become the normal practice, we need to appeal to the Church. Paul and Barnabas decided to take their case to "the apostles and elders in Jerusalem." We need the wisdom of the mother Church and of the Church universal. Here is where norms and laws for all the disciples are gradually reached, through prayer, fasting, consultation and vote!

A *third* expectation is made of us by today's Scriptures: to preserve peace at all costs, without compromising on principles and human rights. Jesus said to his disciples:

Peace is my farewell to you,
my peace is my gift to you;
I do not give it as the world gives peace.

There ought to be an heroic element of patience and hope, of strength and respect in our exercise of peace.

Finally, all our decisions ought to be reached with the vision of heaven before our eyes. Our judgments must lead us and all future generations to our final goal, our eternal home. We need the visions of the book of Revelation to keep a strong light of hope in all that we do and decide.

Through the Spirit we interpret the goals and hopes of Jesus for each new generation of believers. We are responding to this Spirit if we always seek greater peace, prayer, dedication, unity, loyalty, dignity. The emphasis must be on the word "greater."

Prayer:

Let all the nations praise and bless you, O Lord. Grant that we may be your instruments to bring salvation to all the world, at least to the world of men and women, our immediate neighbors. May we be instruments of your Spirit, fired with your love, instructed by your word, united in your Church.

Ascension—"A" "B" "C" Cycles*

Acts 1:1–11. Between Easter and Ascension Jesus instructed the apostles and advised them to "wait ... [for] you will be baptized with the Holy Spirit." Eventually Jesus will return gloriously, the same way by which he ascended from their midst.

Eph 1:17–23. Christ's "fullness fills the universe" and so the Lord distributes "the wealth of his glorious heritage" and "the immeasurable scope of his power in us who believe."

(A) Matt 28:16–20. Stresses the Lord's universal authority and the commission of the apostles to "make disciples of all nations." It was spoken by Jesus in Galilee.

(B) Mark 16:15–20. Emphasizes faith, baptism and the gift of healing.

(c) Luke 24:46–53. Highlights the necessity of Jesus to suffer and the praise of God by the apostles in the Jerusalem temple.

As we compare the various gospel accounts of Jesus' ascension into heaven, we conclude that the evangelists were much more interested in interpreting its meaning than in providing historical data. In fact, the data is sometimes difficult to harmonize. Luke and Mark leave the impression that the ascension might have taken place on Easter itself toward evening. Luke places the event on the Mount of Olives to the east of Jerusalem, while Matthew writes about "the eleven disciples [on] their way to Galilee." Rather than try to fit these details together in a historical tableau, we ought to seek a religious meaning and a pastoral application for each piece of information.

*The feast of the Ascension in some parts of the Church is celebrated on the following Sunday and replaces the readings and other liturgical texts for the Seventh Sunday of Easter.

As we review the theological significance, emphasized with different nuance by each gospel writer, we
have to decide which one has the most practical message
for ourselves within our pastoral setting. We will also notice that the theologies of the different evangelists, while
distinct one from the other, nonetheless harmonize into a
rich appreciation of the *one* Jesus who lived, died and
rose from the dead and ascended into glory for our salvation.

Matthew models his account of the ascension upon
the final verse of the Second Book of Chronicles (2 Chron
36:23). First and Second Chronicles offer a theological
commentary upon the kings of Israel. Very frequently it
quotes from the earlier books of Samuel and Kings, but
always with a unique theological insight (compare 1
Chron 21:1 with 2 Sam 24:1) and a fascination with the
liturgy (compare 1 Chron 16 with 2 Sam 6). Finally,
Chronicles concludes with a world vision, linking the Jerusalem temple with Cyrus' domain of "all the kingdoms
of the earth." In the Hebrew editions of the Bible, Second
Chronicles is the last book and that verse (36:23) the final
words. Matthew, therefore, replaces Cyrus' empire with
the kingdom of heaven established in Jesus.

Through the symbolism of "mountain," Matthew
links Jesus' ascension with other key moments in the
Lord's earthly life: his temptations (4:8), his first major
sermon (5:1) and his transfiguration (17:1). Jesus thus replaces Moses whose mighty work was achieved on a
mountain called Sinai. Both Matthew's gospel and the
reading from Ephesians 1:17–23 for this feast draw our
attention to the gift of healing. God's kingdom on this
earth will be a glorious one with the removal of disease
and every impairment.

The reading from *Mark* is taken from what is called

"the canonical ending," a long conclusion drawn from the other gospels and added after the work of Mark had already been completed. It adds an upbeat to the unfinished state of the original conclusion (16:1–8). Equally inspired as any other part of Mark's gospel, this new ending emphasizes faith, baptism and the apostolic gift of healing.

Luke gathers the major themes of his gospel into the final lines; he also provides a convenient bridge to his other great work, the *Acts of the Apostles,* whose opening lines are read in today's liturgy. Luke frequently points out the necessity of suffering. Another important motif is the role of prayer and liturgy. Luke even uses a special word for Jesus' being "carried up" into heaven. The Greek word normally refers to liturgical sacrifices, being *carried up* as a pleasing fragrance to God (Lev 2:16; 3:5, 11, 14, 16).

We turn to the application of these gospel scenes of Jesus' ascension.

Some of us today are active in the political and economic spheres of life. We are working diligently for social justice, for a proper and happy distribution of world goods, for ways of bringing food and clothing to families, for providing homes and conveniences within the home, etc. *We will want to read and re-read Matthew's gospel,* for we see the presence of Jesus with us always, here on mother earth, with full authority to make our earthly home as happy and peaceful as possible. The glorious ascension of Jesus brings a glow of wonder and joy across our human endeavors.

Others in our midst are born optimists. We turn drab moments of doubt and bewilderment into joy. Where others end on a sad or fearful note, even within the Church, these happy people walk in the ranks of Pope

John XXIII and Pope John Paul I—and smile! They added that canonical ending to Mark's gospel, lest it stop, bewildered and unfinished. They draw statements of joy and triumph from the Scriptures in order to turn sorrow into happiness. They express a new kind of faith and by their optimism attract many to baptism. Not only sorrow but many physical ills are cured. These people, *in the words of Mark's long canonical ending,* "confirm the message through the signs which accompanied them." Everyone then realizes and confesses that Jesus has ascended to glory, for such wonder is reflected in these his servants.

We are grateful for people of prayer. Not only do they exude a quiet strength and a godly awareness, but they also devote much energy to the beauty and dignity of our liturgical services. *Such is the way that Luke's gospel celebrates the feast of the Ascension.* Everything leads to the solemn moment of worship. We gather in the temple, our churches, listen to the Scriptures, learn how suffering becomes a way to glory, and recognize new ways by which the gospel can be preached "to the nations." Yet it all begins "at Jerusalem," the mother church, in continuity with the Lord Jesus, the source of ancient wisdom and good judgment. Each liturgical action lifts us up further in joy and wonder. We are convinced that the Lord Jesus will certainly come again, on the evidence of this glorious moment of worship.

Prayer:

Lord, this day enthrones you in the midst of all human activity. It turns sorrow into joy. It enables us to converge in a moment of worship. You are rising to new glory everywhere in our lives. Grant us the faith to recognize your wonderful presence and to be witnesses of your glory through all the earth.

Seventh Sunday of Easter—"A" Cycle

Acts 1:12–14. After the ascension the remnant of Jesus' disciples gather in the "upstairs room." They include the eleven, Mary the mother of Jesus, other devoted women and men.

1 Pet 4:13–16. Happy are you when you are insulted and suffer for the sake of Christ. Never be ashamed of such treatment.

John 17:1–11. Jesus prays for his disciples, now that he is to depart this earth and be glorified with his heavenly Father. Jesus leaves them in this world, to impart to others the message confided to them by Jesus.

Jesus begins his prayer, in today's selection from John's gospel, with the mysterious exclamation: "Father, the hour has come!" "Hour" has turned out to be a rich, theological term for John, from its first appearance in Jesus' remark to his mother at the marriage feast of Cana: "Woman, how does this concern of yours involve me? My hour has not yet come" (John 2:4). From many passages in John's gospel (*i.e.*, 7:6, 30; 8:20; 12:23, 27; 13:1), we begin to understand that "hour" or "time" includes simultaneously Jesus' Passion, death, resurrection and ascension.

In today's gospel, Jesus associates his "hour" with his glorification:

Father, the hour has come!
Give glory to your son
that your Son may give glory to you.

Peacefully, in this passage, Jesus promises his continued presence with his disciples and particularly his intercession for them: "For these I pray ... for these you have given me." Jesus can be assured that his disciples will keep the word, that is, hand on faithfully and integrally the teaching which the Father entrusted to him. As he announces that his hour has come, Jesus speaks from a heart tranquil and at rest.

At another time, however, his words reveal a different attitude. In the presence of two apostles, Philip and Andrew, Jesus' self-composure gives way to the very human reaction of fear:

> My soul is troubled now,
> yet what should I say—
> Father, save me from this hour?
> But it was for this that I came to this hour.
> Father, glorify your name!"

Many scholars consider this passage in John's gospel a theological commentary upon Jesus' agony in the garden; another reflective interpretation is found in Hebrews 5:7-10.

As a matter of fact, when Jesus' "hour" came and he was lifted up upon the cross (John 8:20, 28), his disciples shared in the troubled heart of Jesus. As we learn in the first reading for today, they secluded themselves in the "upstairs room" and waited in prayer. They did not know what to make of the final week of Jesus' life on earth. Even his appearance to them over forty days since his resurrection on Easter Sunday did not allay their fears and certainly did not explain what it all meant. They prayed, but that in itself was insufficient. Only after the coming of the Holy Spirit, in answer to their prayers and to Jesus' promise, did they summon the strength to appear publicly and show themselves "full of joy that they had been judged worthy of ill-treatment for the sake of the Name" (Acts 5:41).

By perseverance in prayer, we too hope to grow into that attitude of deep confidence which we read in Peter's first epistle: "Rejoice, insofar as you share Christ's sufferings .... Happy are you when you are insulted for the sake of Christ, for then God's Spirit in its glory has come to rest on you." If our first reaction to sorrow and disappointment does not measure up to Peter's instruction, we ought to remind ourselves that not even Peter was equal to it, immediately after Jesus' Passion, resurrection and ascension. For that matter we can reverently go back to Jesus, whose own soul was troubled in anticipation of his death.

If we are not ready for Peter's advice to "Rejoice!" and be "Happy!" we can profitably listen to his other advice: "See to it that none of you suffers for being a murderer, a thief, a malefactor, or a destroyer of another's rights." When tragedy hits, we are often inclined to blame others and to drag them down with ourselves. We are tempted to meet violence with violence. We tend to destroy the rights of others. When Peter rushed forward to cut off the ear of Malchus, Jesus replied: "Put your sword back in its sheath. Am I not to drink the cup the Father has given me?" (John 18:10-11) We too must drink the cup. We must permit God's will to run its full course. If we do not understand, then we must persevere, waiting in prayer. At times, to do anything is to do wrong!

In any case, Peter also advises us: "If anyone suffers for being a Christian, that person ought not to be ashamed but rather glorify God in virtue of that name." Confused as we may be about the cause and the purpose of our suffering, convinced that we are afflicted unjustly (and that knowledge is presumably accurate), unable to give reasons for our hopes, still we should possess deeply within us a remembrance of Jesus' words: "For these I pray ... for they are really yours." This petition by Jesus to his heavenly Father imparts an interior strength, a conviction of faith, so that even if we are publicly humiliated, we are still not ashamed. In the prophecy of the Suffering Servant, we are told:

> I gave my back to those who beat me,
>   my cheeks to those who plucked my beard;
> My face I did not shield
>   from *the shame of being spit upon.*
> The Lord God is my help,
>   therefore *I am not put to shame.*

Isaiah plays on the word "shame." He was shamed in the sight of others but not in his own eyes nor in the eyes of God. He bore "the *shame* of being spit upon [without being] put to *shame!*"

Prayer:

Lord God, you promised not to leave us orphaned but to remain with us always. Be with us in our confusion and disappointment when we do not know what to do. Grant that we may hear your call to silence and prayer and that we will withdraw to our "upstairs room." Lead us to that moment when we will glory in the privilege of sharing your sufferings. As we remain within your troubled heart, our heart will grow in peace with yours.

Seventh Sunday of Easter—"B" Cycle

Acts 1:15–17, 20–26. Matthias is chosen to take the place of Judas Iscariot, so as to reconstitute the "twelve."

1 John 4:11–16. We must possess the same love for one another that God has for us. God's love is so surprising and so overwhelming that we accept it on faith.

John 17:11–19. Jesus prays for the protection of his followers and for their dedication to his word and to truth.

Today's Scripture readings place us in those critical days between Ascension and Pentecost. Jesus has left the disciples to make their own decisions and to arrive at their identity without his immediate, visible presence. The disciples of Jesus are beginning that long and difficult trek, first of adjusting themselves within Judaism and eventually of considering themselves to be the true heirs of Israel's promises from God. We can direct our own reflections in several important ways: to explore the role of the Church in its evolving structure and styles of authority; or to examine the Church's way of interpreting Scripture; or finally, to observe dramatic leaps within the continuity of Israel-to-Church.

The historical setting is provided by the first reading from Acts. The remnant of Jesus' disciples are still gathered in the "upstairs room" (see the Seventh Sunday of Easter—"A" Cycle). Peter is visibly the head of the group. He took the initiative to stand up and begin the negotiations that led to a successor for Judas Iscariot. The other apostles must also be present, for the whole point of the action is to reconstitute them as "twelve." We learn from a previous passage in Acts that the one hundred and twenty persons in the "upstairs room" included both men and women, with prominent attention given to Mary, the mother of Jesus (Acts 1:14).

This group of disciples already consider themselves in a direct line with Judaism, not only with the twelve apostles, corresponding to the twelve tribes, but also with the one hundred and twenty members (12 x 10), the minimum number for the Jewish Sanhedrin or governing body. Yet the disciples of Jesus are already beginning to separate from their parent religion; they have their own "sanhedrin." The spirit of Jesus too is introducing a new style of interaction; this sanhedrin is called "brothers," a frequent name in the Church for the men and women who form the Christian community.

The "brothers and sisters" want to maintain not only their relationship with Judaism but also their identity as followers of Jesus. Because Jesus had gathered twelve apostles, they too must consist of "twelve" at their center of government. They explain the loss of one of their members, Judas Iscariot, by referring to the Scriptures, Psalms 69:26 and 109:8. The citations are drawn from the Greek, not the Hebrew, in order to apply more directly to the question of Judas. There is a curious touch here in the use of the Greek word *episkopē*, to translate "encampment", in Psalm 69:29, "Let his encampment be desolate," and our mind runs forward to the day when the *episkopē* is considered a continuation of the twelve apostles!

In any case, this application to Judas could never have been imagined ahead of time. The ancient Scriptures, therefore, are interpreted in the light of Jesus and Church life. Once the connection is thus made, then the Bible throws light upon our contemporary life. Scripture is not so much a quarry to obtain rocks for arguments but a hidden depth from which to explore the mystery of God.

The Church did not wait for a direct revelation, but chose Matthias by lot. Yet its final decision comes as much from the Holy Spirit as from the human agents within the Church. Later at the Council of Jerusalem their resolution of a difficult theological problem, reached after long debate, is introduced with the phrase: "It is the decision of the Holy Spirit, and ours too . . ." (Acts 15:28).

Another difficult adjustment has to be made when Paul is called immediately by Jesus to be an apostle, equal in all ways with the Twelve (Gal 1:11–19). The category of "Twelve" collapses as a literal fulfillment of Jesus' earthly group of apostles; it has to be taken symbolically. Like the Old Testament Scriptures, the Church's decision is re-interpreted.

As already mentioned, the company of the Christian disciples are called "brothers." If the Bible were being written today, the phrase would be "brothers and sisters," for such was the actual composition of the 120 people in the upstairs room. The emphasis is upon family, upon loyalty, upon a bond of love. Organization and authority are to be conspicuous for their gentleness, concern, trust and most of all their love. We read in John's first letter:

> Beloved,
> if God has loved us so,
> we must have the same love for one another.
> If we love one another,
> God dwells in us.
> The way we know we remain in him

and he in us
is that he has given us of his Spirit.

As we turn to the gospel reading for this Sunday, we are made to realize the difficulty of maintaining this family love and trust as the most visible characteristic of Jesus' disciples. Jesus prays:

> O Father most holy,
> protect them.
> Guard them from the evil one.

This world rebellion against God and against his followers is one of the biblical expressions for "original sin." Under these circumstances a person would normally want to forget all about love and fight back. At least, the sense of trust would be stretched to the breaking point and we would become ever more suspicious of others. We take on these defensive attitudes in order to protect the truth confided to us by Jesus. As this happens, the "brotherhood" tends to dissolve and to become some sort of secular organization.

Love we accept on faith, and we can never defend it with simply rational motivation and human means. What we are at the depth of ourselves as brothers and sisters of the Lord Jesus is the most basic dogma of our faith. Faith can never be proven unless by the intuitive ways we project a goodness and a loyalty beyond the power of words and sentences to convey.

Prayer:

Lord, grant that we may always grow as Church in the love that makes us who we are, your brothers and sisters. Make the exercise of your authority, like Peter's, one of trust. Help us to turn continually to the Scriptures to be enlightened in your truth. May all the world know that you abide in our midst by the love that we manifest.

Seventh Sunday of Easter—"C" Cycle

Acts 7:55–60. Luke models the story of Stephen's martyrdom upon the passion narrative of Jesus' death.

Rev 22:12–14, 16–17, 20. From heaven Jesus promises to come soon. The Church in glory as well as the Church on earth replies: *"Marana tha*—Come, Our Lord!"

John 17:20–26. Jesus prays for future members of his community, that they may be one "as you, Father, are in me, and I am in you."

At first, the thrust of the first two readings, from Acts and Revelation, seems to clash with the spirit of John. While John presumes a long history of future members for the Church, Acts and Revelation refer to a quick manifestation of Jesus. These two works, moreover, are dominated by the fulfillment of prophecy. The book of Revelation looks to the Old Testament; Acts turns to the gospel account of Jesus' death.

The continual weaving of Old Testament passages into the book of Revelation heightens the sense of imminent fulfillment. When this use of prophecy is woven into an apocalyptic account of persecution and the imminent dissolution of the world, the second coming of the Lord Jesus becomes all the more pressing. Delays can hardly be tolerated any longer.

Many phrases echo the Hebrew Scriptures, particularly the books of Isaiah, Ezekiel and Daniel. The book of Isaiah increases its momentum, as one section follows another and we arrive at the vision of the new heaven and the new earth (Is 65:17). The prophet Ezekiel is granted overpowering visions and he falls with his face against the ground (Ez 2:1). The book of Daniel represents the apocalyptic, visionary style full blown, and we are terrified at the visions of the beast, of Jerusalem smashed to the ground, of the martyred saints coming like the son of man upon the clouds. Such terrifying tensions cannot be sustained any longer and the seer on the island of Patmos (Rev 1:9) cries out in the ancient Aramaic phrase: "*Marana tha*—Come, Our Lord!"

We too, at this point of the Church year, expect the Holy Spirit to come any moment. The feast of Pentecost is only one week away. Rightly we can expect wonderful changes in our lives and in our Church. The walls will collapse at the force of the whirlwind! Liturgically we are reliving many other moments in our lives when our faith is strained to the breaking point and we feel that we cannot endure the pain any longer. Our entire world may seem to be falling apart, we are facedown against the dirt of the earth, only a new heaven and a new earth are worth consideration. The book of Revelation assures us that it is all right to cry out in desperation. There is nothing wrong, and it is certainly not an illusion, to hear all the saints of heaven joining us in the prayer, "*Marana tha*."

> The Spirit [that is, the prophets] and the Bride [that is, the saints in glory, God's beloved ones] say, "Come!" Let him who hears [all the members of the Church, in heaven and on earth] answer, "Come!" Let him who is thirsty [all of us under persecution and longing for paradise] come forward; let all who desire it accept the gift of life-giving water.

Those were times of severe temptation and crushing persecution, and they are being endured today in some parts of the Church. There were other times, still under persecution, when the response of God's saints is much calmer, as we see in the martyrdom of St. Stephen. The narrative is like a peaceful meditation upon the narrative of Jesus' death:

Stephen, filled with the Holy Spirit	Luke 4:1 before the struggle with Satan Jesus is filled with the Holy Spirit.
looked to the sky above and saw the glory of God, and Jesus standing at God's right hand	Luke 22:69 Son of Man . . . at the right hand of the power of God
the onlookers held their hands over ears and rushed at him	Matt 26:65 the high priest tore his robes: "He has blasphemed!"
dragged him outside the city	Luke 20:15 dragged outside the vineyard
witness	Luke 22:71 no further need of witnesses
Lord Jesus, receive my spirit	Luke 23:46 Father, into your hands
Lord, do not hold this sin against them	Luke 23:34 Father, forgive them

Acts transforms a moment of horrible violence into a space of contemplative prayer, peace and forgiveness. This kind of reflection requires much time. To memorize the Scriptures and speak their words in our own tragedies, to relive them peacefully even when our world is falling apart—all this is possible because Jesus prayed for his community, the Church. As we find in today's gospel:

I do not pray for my disciples alone.
I pray also for those who will believe in me
through their word,

that all may be one
as you, Father, are in me, and I in you;
I pray that they may be [one] in us
that the world may believe that you sent me.

Only by a strong unity, of one generation of believers with the next, of one part of the Church with the other, of the persecuted Church with the Church at peace, of the Church falling apart with the Church firmly knit together in love and in truth, can we absorb the Scriptures into our system and speak their language. In this way we support the agonizing who cry out desperately: "*Marana tha.*" We are assisted by the peaceful contemplatives who feel the presence of Jesus already in their painful moment of death. In this way we show the love of Jesus in our midst.

Prayer:

Lord, in this moment of prayer you have come into our midst. Sustain in us this moment of prayer and allow us to remain forever in your presence. Then you will have already answered the cry from our hearts: "*Marana tha.*"

Pentecost Vigil—"A" "B" "C" Cycles*

Gen 11:1–9. The incident of the Tower of Babel. Due to pride and revolt against God, the one language of the human race was scrambled and thereafter no one understood anyone else.

Ex 19:3–8, 16–20. After an assurance that Israel was God's "special possession, dearer to me than all other

---

*For the first reading there is a choice between passages from Genesis, Exodus, Ezekiel or Joel. The second reading is taken from Romans 8 and the gospel from John 7.

people," the Lord came down on Mount Sinai amid thunder and trumpet blasts.

Ez 37:1–14. The vision of bones scattered over the bleak fields. The Spirit joins those bones together, covers them with sinews, flesh and skin, and breathes life into the new creature so that Israel becomes a new people.

Joel 3:1–5. The Spirit will be poured out on all humankind amid wonders in the heavens and on earth.

Rom 8:22–27. All creation groans in travail, and the Spirit makes intercession for us with groaning, searching our heart.

John 7:37–39. From within the heart of Jesus' disciples, rivers of living water, that is, the Spirit, shall flow, once Jesus is glorified.

In the Scriptures there is never anything soft or gentle about the Spirit. The Hebrew word, *ruah,* can just as easily be translated "a mighty wind" as in the opening verses of Genesis in the *New American Bible.* The Spirit of the Lord comes upon the warrior judges like Jephthah (Judg 11:29) and Samson (Judg 14:6, 19). Jephthah then rushed off to battle and Samson tore a lion to pieces! We are told on another occasion that the Spirit of the Lord "rushed upon Samson and he became very angry" against the Ammonites who were threatening to invade and oppress Israel. In a more religious way the Spirit of the Lord rushed upon Saul as he met a band of charismatic prophets and as the text says: "changed him into another man" (1 Sam 10:6).

This overwhelming power of the Spirit shows up as well in the biblical attempts to describe such awesome moments as the covenant at Mount Sinai, the assembly of the Israelites after the tortuous days of exile, or the inauguration of the new covenant in the messianic age.

These biblical passages from Exodus, Ezekiel and Joel are important because St. Luke, in composing the account of Pentecost in the Acts of the Apostles, will draw upon them as well as upon still other passages like Genesis 11:1–9 and the scrambling of languages at the Tower of Babel. Even if a great deal of symbolic language has been woven into each of these accounts, we must always ask: symbolic of what? The answer cannot avoid the conviction that stupendous power accompanies the Spirit of God.

This irresistible strength in pursuit of a goal—if the Spirit is from God—becomes an awesome power of evil—if the spirit is diabolical. Actually in the opening chapter of Genesis, the *ruah* or spirit which "swept over the waters" roared through a black abyss of chaos. Light had not yet been created. The imagery behind this story is to be found in the ancient myths of Mesopotamia in which good and evil gods fought one another. In Genesis then *ruah* originally meant a raging force of chaos which God tames and puts to full benefit for his human family. God's word put order and harmony into the universe.

Another instance of the spirit of evil is found in the account of the Tower of Babel. The confusing of languages in the human race meant that people no longer understood one another, became fearful and jealous, and then defensive and hostile, finally aggressive in attacking the enemy.

The classical prophets like Isaiah began to recognize the *interior* presence of the spirit. It will rest upon the seemingly dead stump of the "tree" of Jesse, David's father, and new gentle life will bud forth (Is 11:1). By means of this image Isaiah announces both the destruction of the house or dynasty of David because of its pride and sinfulness as well as its mysterious revival in the dis-

tant future. The Spirit becomes all the more invisible—
yet still as strong and powerful as ever—when it comes to
abide with the Suffering Servant of the Lord (Is 42:1)
who in turn brings glad tidings to the lowly, healing the
afflicted (Is 61:1).

The New Testament continues this process of seeing
the all-powerful Spirit of the Lord, deeply imbedded
within the heart of the believer. It stirs hopes and long-
ings, groanings so vibrant that they resonate through the
universe. Paul wrote in Romans: "all creation groans and
is in agony even until now" as we who have the Spirit
"groan inwardly as we await the redemption of our bod-
ies."

This interior Spirit is also our teacher in the ways of
prayer:

> The Spirit too helps us in our weakness for we
> do not know how to pray as we ought ... He
> who searches hearts knows what the Spirit
> means, for the Spirit intercedes for the saints as
> God himself wills.

Even if the spirit is more and more interior, its power remains as vigorous as ever—as it imparts conviction, irre-
versible hopes, courage in believing what others call impossible or totally foolish, openheartedness to embrace
the world, in fact the universe in all its wondrous possibilities.

Jesus promises that this Spirit will flow from the
heart of the believer like streams of living water, to transform the desert into paradise. The same text of St. John
also gives us a hint of the fearful cost to Jesus. John adds:
"There was, of course, no Spirit as yet, since Jesus had
not yet been glorified." Glory for John meant the coura-

geous but gruesome way of the cross and crucifixion, followed by the stupendous way to heaven through the resurrection and ascension. (See the Seventh Sunday of Easter—"A" Cycle.) For the Spirit to be imparted upon the disciples, Jesus must accept, actively with all the strength of his soul, the will of his Father that he die for ungrateful sinners. Jesus must struggle with all the forces of chaos as he passed through the darkness of death, before the new creation be achieved.

Prayer:

Lord, we pray for your Spirit, knowing that the cost will be dear and the consequences overwhelming. We earnestly implore you to send your mighty Holy Spirit into the depth of ourselves, into the heart of your Church. We accept the consequences, for it is our glory to follow Jesus' way of the cross and our reward his way to heaven through the resurrection and ascension.

Pentecost Sunday—"A" "B" "C" Cycles

Acts 2:1–11. The awesome descent of the Spirit, so that all are caught up in wonder and hear the marvels of God spoken in their own tongue.

1 Cor 12:3–7, 12–13. There are different gifts but the same Spirit. In the one Spirit all of us were baptized into one body [and] have been given to drink of the one Spirit.

John 20:19–23. Jesus breathed upon the disciples, gathered together in a locked room; he conferred the Holy Spirit and the power of forgiving sin.

The account of Pentecost in the Acts of the Apostles orchestrates many of the stupendous theophanies of the

Old Testament. Other texts, referring to the division of people and their reunion, are also alluded to. Some of these passages were available to us in the mass for the vigil of Pentecost. We can draw up at least the following parallels:

rushing of the Spirit	as upon the judges or in Isaiah 66:25
fire and earthquake	as on Mount Sinai (Ex 19)
division of peoples according to languages and their reunion	Tower of Babel (Gen 11)
filled with the Spirit	as the spirit reunited the bones in Ezekiel's vision (Ex 37)
nations of the earth	united under Noah's son in Genesis 10, but scattered at the Tower of Babel (Gen 11)
giving of the new law	gift of the Mosaic law, celebrated on the Jewish feast of Weeks, their Pentecost

Pentecost is not less real if Luke calls upon some of the most vigorous symbols of the Hebrew Bible to describe it. It means that it is all the more real, because human language has collapsed at the task given to it and the author must resort to a cacophony of unusual passages.

The Spirit grants the power of *peace* and *union*. Even in Luke's account, Pentecost unified the most unusual texts and episodes of earlier times. Each seems so strong and so independent in its own right in the Old Testament, that one wonders how anyone would dare to match them all together.

In the second reading for this Pentecost Sunday, Paul details the many gifts of the Spirit. This is especially true if one reads the entire Chapter 12: gifts to be apostles, prophets, teachers, miracle workers, healers, assistants, administrators, speaking in tongues! These abundant and wonderful gifts of the Spirit, each to be admired and exercised, disintegrated into many deep divisions in the Corinthian church. Over and over, Paul returns to Jesus' expectation of unity and charity. Finally, in desperation he writes: "If I speak with angelic tongues . . . possess the gift of prophecy . . . comprehend mysteries . . . have faith strong enough to move mountains, *but have not love, I am nothing.*"

The Corinthian church was divided between Apollos, Cephas, Paul and Christ (I Cor 1:10–12), between the wealthy and the poor (I Cor 11:17–22), between Jews and Greeks (as we note in today's epistle), between slaves and free (again in today's epistle).

In many ways, as the Corinthian church makes very clear, Pentecost did not remove problems, it caused more difficulties. The greater the presence of the Spirit, the more gifted are God's people. And gifts tend to make people jealous, defensive and eventually aggressive.

With good reason then when Jesus breathed upon the apostles and said: "Receive the Holy Spirit," he simultaneously granted the power to forgive sins. Wherever there exist the abundant gifts of the Spirit, there will have to be readiness to forgive.

Jesus also showed the apostles his hands and his side, accompanying the gesture with the words, "Peace be with you." The marks of the nails and the imprint of the spear point out the need to suffer for one another. This suffering, modeled upon that of Jesus on the cross, means a strong attitude of patient endurance. How much we need to be patient with the wonderful gifts of other people. They are too good! Unfortunately, goodness is directed along a single narrow line, and remains unbalanced and hostile. As a result, Paul must remind his readers in First Corinthians: "God is a God, not of confusion, but of peace" (14:33). The gifts of the Spirit, through a common bond of forgiveness, patience and long suffering, will begin to balance off. Each gift will be seen in relation to the gifts of other people.

Pentecost seeks to create a church of exceptionally gifted people, each member brilliant in his or her own ways, each one necessary that the others turn out to be balanced and well put together. Our Church, due to the gifts of the Spirit, is by no means a community of mediocre people, with vague goals and indifferent expectations. On the contrary, our hopes are the highest, our talents the best, our strengths unbeatable. This means that our problems are superhuman and can be solved only by turning to the wounded Jesus on the cross.

We do not fear the gifts of the Spirit at Pentecost, if we are united in prayer and in shared ambitions. We have to be big enough to see the sins and offenses of others as somehow the excesses of their good gifts, out of proper relationship with the rest of the community. We must always be ready to forgive in the name of an all loving God. We must always remember that our finest gifts can turn against us and become our worst sins, if we do not seek a strong bond of peace with all our neighbors.

Prayer:

Come, Holy Spirit! Come, Father and Mother of the poor! Come, our sweet refreshment, our solace in the midst of woe, our light in darkness. Healer of our wounds, dew upon our dryness, warmth for our cold hearts. Bring the orphans home that all our gifts of life form one family within your Church.

BIBLICAL INDEX

(Asterisk indicates a more extended reflection.)

231

TOPICAL INDEX

237